THE
organic
beer
GUIDE

First published in 2002

10 9 8 7 6 5 4 3 2 1

A CIP catalogue record for this book is available from the British Library

ISBN 1 84222 575 8

Managing Editor: Martin Corteel
Assistant Editor: David Ballheimer
Project Art Direction: Jim Lockwood
Production: Sarah Corteel
Designed by Maria Lamle

Printed in Singapore

Author's Acknowledgements

Thanks to: in France, Aymeric Gillet and Gwenaël Samotyj of ATPUB for their dedicated work in tracking down small breweries producing organic beer; in Austria, the distinguished beer writer Conrad Seidl, who helped with information about German producers and translated from websites in German; in the United States, Seven Bridges Co-Operative for identifying brewers of organic beer, and writer Greg Kitsock, editor of *Mid-Atlantic Brewing News*, whose major article in *All About Beer* magazine on organic beer in North America was enlightening; in Britain, Nigel Jones and Beer Barons for help, advice and beer samples.

THE
organic
beer
GUIDE

ROGER PROTZ

CARLTON
BOOKS

How the guide is organised

The Organic Beer Guide is broken down into countries and, with the exception of the United States, concentrates on beers that are available for sale in Great Britain. Where known, we list without tasting notes beers in France and Germany that are not exported but may be found on visits to those countries.

We name the organic certification bodies in mainland European countries and the US. In Britain, the certification bodies for organic beer are Organic Farmers and Growers (OF&G), which also appears on labels as UK 2, and the Soil Association, also known as UK 5. OF&G permits an opt-out that allows brewers to call beers organic if they use five per cent of non-organic material, usually hops. The Soil Association does not have such an opt-out.

Contents

Introduction

"Man's greatest single task today is to develop in himself the power of non-violence. Everything he does violently, for example, in agriculture, could also be done relatively non-violently, that is gently, organically, patiently adapted to the rhythms of life. The true task of all further research and development is surely to devise non-violent methods of reaching the results which man requires for his existence on earth."

– E.F. Schumacher, 1967
Schumacher, a German-born British economist,
is best-known for his book Small Is Beautiful.

Every year, when the small green plants that give bitterness to beer have been safely harvested, and autumn mists gather on the hills, valleys and skeletal hop trellises of Kent and Worcestershire, England's hop farmers gather in a London pub for a well-deserved celebration. They enjoy a hearty meal washed down with beers that blossom and boom with the unique aromas and flavours imparted by English hops.

In the 1990s, the farmers opened their annual dinner to a few beer writers sympathetic to the hop growers' cause. They found they had a cuckoo in the nest. When I first tentatively raised the question of organic hops, I felt I had stepped into one of those celebrated H.M. Bateman cartoons, where posh gentlemen lose their monocles in pop-eyed dismay at an appalling social gaffe performed by one of their number.

The farmers told me there was no demand for organic beer, a claim that flew in the face of the considerable success of the Caledonian Brewery's Golden Promise. They said that most organic malt and hops presented to brewers were "rubbish". And they stressed that I had no concept of the difficulty they faced in growing conventional hops, let alone organic ones.

Their opposition was a challenge. I became determined to study the hop industry in order to understand the problems faced by farmers, and to see whether their opposition to converting to organic production was open to question.

My interest in organic food and drink was fuelled by a number of agricultural catastrophes at the turn of the 21st century. Salmonella, e-coli, BSE and its human variant CJD scarred the 1990s. And then in 2001 the dreadful plague of foot-and-mouth created funeral pyres the length and breadth of the country as millions of animals – many of them perfectly fit and healthy – were slaughtered. Britain, for many months, resembled not so much a modern, civilised society as a nightmare plucked from the pages of Dante's *Inferno*.

Farming seems set on a destructive course. Land is dominated by "agribusiness", giant rural corporations that, over the past 30 years, have ripped out hedgerows and woods – natural habitats for birds and insects – in order to turn land into prairies fit for oil seed rape. The philosophy of agribusiness has forced hapless herbivore cattle and sheep to consume the minced-up remains of other animals, including their own kind.

The use of chemicals – fertilisers, herbicides, pesticides and animal steroids – proliferates. Rachel Carson's seminal work, *Silent Spring*, published in 1962, led to a worldwide ban on DDT. A ban is not the same as eradication. Many of us who grew up in the 1950s and 60s will still have minute traces of DDT in our bodies. Carson, an environmentalist before the term was invented, was a lone voice among scientists at the time. She wrote about the importance of understanding the "whole fabric" of nature, and the cumulative dangers of minute daily exposure to synthetic chemicals.

Newer chemicals have taken the place of DDT. 100,000 synthetic chemicals have been released into the environment. They concentrate in food and accumulate in the human body. Each one of us carries 500 man-made chemicals in our bodies. There is now a growing view, backed by scientific research, that points to a palpable link between chemicals in the food chain and the epidemic of cancer in Britain, "sexual cancers" in particular: breast, ovaries and testes. (By a terrible irony, Rachel Carson died of breast cancer just two years after *Silent Spring* appeared.)

In 2001, I watched in disbelief as a plane dive-bombed fields of vegetables in Lincolnshire, spraying them with chemicals. The plane circled repeatedly over the fields, a mist of chemicals hanging in the air. I discovered shortly after that experience that Lincolnshire, one of Britain's major agricultural counties, has a level of breast cancer 40 per cent higher than the national average.

Lindane, which is now being phased out within the European Union, is an organochlorine widely used in agriculture. It impairs animal hormones and causes breast cancer in humans. It has been found in analysis of human breast milk, along with 300 other chemicals. In 1996, more than 30 per cent of all cows' milk had varying levels of Lindane. Just as with DDT, Lindane may be phased out but it will remain in animals and humans for years. There has been a massive increase in cancer in the industrialised societies. Twenty years ago, one in five people suffered from cancer. Today the ratio is one in three, and it's predicted to rise to one in two. Even when individual chemicals are pronounced safe there is little research into how pesticides work in concert in the human body. Fruit and vegetables contain multiple residues: it's known as "the witch's brew effect".

Agricultural chemicals are not confined to the food we eat. They are subject to drift. Chemicals may be sprayed on a few acres of land, but they are carried by the breeze far and wide. The same is true with genetically modified plants, fruits, vegetables and cereals. Pollen from GM land is carried by the breeze, birds and insects to other areas. It is perfectly possible for a farmer to convert his land to organic production, and then find his produce infected by chemical sprays and GM pollen from neighbouring farms.

Genetic modification is the ultimate agricultural horror. Global giants are perverting nature by breeding food in which genes have been transferred across the species, such as potatoes injected with genes from fish. Genetic modification has been developed by such global giants as Monsanto and Novartis as a response to growing concerns about agricultural chemicals.

The giants' claim that GM food requires lower levels of herbicides and is therefore good for the environment is a specious one. For example, the natural toxin Bacillus thuringiensis (Bt) is widely used in organic farming to control pests such as caterpillars. It degrades rapidly in sunlight. On the other hand, when Bt is genetically transferred to such crops as potatoes and maize it doesn't degrade but stays permanently in the plants. This enables pests to develop resistance to Bt and for the toxin to be transferred to other plants. A recent study in Germany found herbicide-resistant genes in bees that had been feeding on pollen from GM oil seed rape.

Writing in *Organic: A New Way of Eating*, William Black says, "There are other concerns regarding herbicide-resistant genes. Monsanto, the creator of one of the most widely applied herbicides – Roundup – has also been marketing genetically engineered Roundup-resistant soya beans for several years, much of it on the spurious environmental claim that it will mean lower herbicide use. The principle here of course is that the soya with resistance will survive when sprayed with Roundup when other plants will not.

"Quite why this ever suggested lower herbicide use beats me, for what is happening is that some farmers are spraying the crop with about three times as much Roundup as before, and Monsanto can happily profit from both seed and herbicide sales. As well as actually encouraging higher herbicide use, it has been shown that there are now higher residual herbicide levels in the resistant soya bean as well."

There has been massive resistance to GM food in Britain. The *Daily Mail* describes GM produce as "Frankenstein food". When the most socially conservative newspaper in Britain can react in this way, it is clear it speaks for a large constituency. Yet while minimal support is given by the government to organic farming, large areas of land (larger than at first admitted) have been set aside for GM experiments.

Working with nature

I found, when I visited Peter Hall's farm in Kent (see Hops section), that organic hops can be successfully grown and harvested without the use of chemicals. His approach encourages nature to tackle the problems of pests and disease. The argument from conventional farmers – that organic farming cannot guarantee safety from pests and disease, and that lower yields result – doesn't stand up to scrutiny. Millions of gallons of chemicals are sprayed every year on hop farms, yet the farmers regularly complain the harvest has been blighted by red spider mites and damson hop aphids.

The reason is that the pests develop resistance to the sprays, the sprays are made stronger and harsher, and eventually the pests develop resistance to those sprays, too. As Jonathan Swift wrote, "So naturalists observe, a flea hath smaller fleas that on him prey; And these have smaller fleas to bite 'em, And so proceed ad infinitum". The sprays not only cover the hops but also the bines that have roots in the earth. So the chemicals are carried directly into the soil and indirectly as a result of "chemical drift".

The only way in which organic hops can create a bigger yield is, to state the blindingly obvious, to grow more of them. Before the post-World War Two "cheap food" revolution, English hops were grown either organically or with much less reliance on chemicals. Far bigger volumes of beer were consumed between the two world wars than today. As a result, hop growing was a bigger agricultural activity in that period.

I have read many accounts of hop picking in the 1930s, including the graphic descriptions in George Orwell's novel *A Clergyman's Daughter*, but have found little or nothing about harvests destroyed by pests and disease. The long hours for low wages enjoyed [sic] by Cockney and Brummie hop pickers in the 1930s suggest that hops grew in abundance without the aid of organo-phosphates, which didn't exist at the time. They were invented by the Nazis as poison gas.

Peter Hall, who grows conventional hops as well as organic Target, believes his organic ones taste better. As hops give superb aroma and flavour to beer as well as bitterness, it is clearly better to allow hops to impart those qualities without chemical impediments.

Geetie Singh, co-founder of a small group of all-organic pubs in London (see Heroes of Organics), says that organic beer doesn't give drinkers hangovers. Dedicated research on my part has failed to justify this claim. On the other hand, regular visits to the Munich Oktoberfest, the world's biggest beer festival, have proved that drinking beers made to the exacting standards of the Reinheitsgebot – the Purity Law – does not produce that "I wish I were dead" feeling the following morning. German beers can be made only from malted barley and wheat, hops, yeast and water. No cheaper cereals, sugars or chemicals that produce fake froth and longer shelf life are permitted. Such beers are not, in the main, made from organic materials. But the Germans have a head start. Their belief in purity should convince them of the need to go the extra mile and use ingredients produced without chemicals.

The taste and enjoyment of beer is purely subjective. It is impossible to say whether or not organic beer "tastes better" than conventional beer. A craft beer will taste better than a bland American global lager for the simple reason that one is made from the best-quality ingredients while the other will have malt diluted by corn and rice, the most minimal hop content, and chemicals added to prolong active life.

It is not the aim of this guide to claim that craft-brewed conventional beer will harm you. The most dangerous thing in your glass is the alcohol. By the time malt has been thoroughly mixed or "mashed" with water from which the impurities have been removed, the sweet extract vigorously boiled with hops, and the hopped extract fermented by yeast, it would take a herbicide or pesticide of remarkable tenacity to survive. On the other hand, never forget the infamous supermarket lettuce that had been washed 16 times, but still contained chemical traces.

I am concerned not only about the taste of beer, but by the damage done to the environment by the use of chemicals. An organic beer may not necessarily taste better than a conventional one, but its production will have done far less harm to the world we live in.

Cider-maker Ivor Dunkerton (see Heroes of Organics) says, in the 20 years he has lived and worked in Herefordshire, "the wildife has been decimated. Curlews and yellowhammers have disappeared completely and I haven't seen a hare in years."

In the Pacific North-west of the United States, Crayne Horton invests some of the income from his organic Fish Tail Brewery into cleaning local rivers of nitrates in order that wild salmon can return. It's the chemical cocktail used by conventional farming that destroys the natural habitats for the very birds and insects that would normally kill the pests that feed on plants, fruit and vegetables.

The damage to the environment destroys essential links in the food chain. The nitrates that pour from the fields of East Anglia into the Norfolk Broads have turned the waters turbid and kill the organisms on which fish feed. As fish die out so, too, do the birds that feed on them. Many of Britain's bird species are disappearing, and it is birds that eat the pests that are the enemy of the farmer.

The absurdity of the distorted values of modern agriculture can be seen at first hand in the area of barley production. Barley is the essential raw material for making beer, and brewers want barley that is low in nitrogen. Too much nitrogen can impede a sound fermentation, and result in a haze in the finished beer, which makes it unacceptable to drinkers. Yet farmers dose their fields with nitrates in order to increase yields, apparently oblivious to the brewers' needs.

The problems facing brewers who want organic hops and malt confront craft cider-makers on an even greater scale. Thousands of acres of trees bearing traditional cider apples and perry pears have been grubbed up in the past 20 or 30 years. As the two giants that dominate cider-making in Britain have switched their production to largely tasteless filtered, pasteurised and artificially carbonated "ciderades", they have stopped using traditional apples and pears, and now buy imported fruit concentrates from as far away as Turkey. If they use proper but conventional apples, they will use some of the most chemically sprayed fruit in the country: the average British-grown apple is sprayed no fewer than 40 times.

Until the rise of craft cider-makers, it was uneconomic for farmers to grow cider apples and perry pears. It takes several years to develop new orchards, and several more years for the fruit to reach an acceptable standard. In 1996, according to SUSTAIN, the Alliance for Better Food and Farming, Britain imported 434,000 tonnes of apples, of which more than 200,000 tonnes came from outside the European Union. Since 1970, more than 60 per cent of Britain's orchards have been grubbed up. Transport by plane is not only expensive, but adds to pollution and degradation of the atmosphere. A plane uses 15,839 kilojoules per metric tonne of goods transported per kilometre. Trains use 677, boats 423, and trucks 2,890.

The cost

The chief complaint from consumers against organic food and drink is the cost. With only three per cent of Britain's agricultural land given over to organic production, it is a low-batch, low-yield, labour-intensive business. The percentage is even lower in the United States. Organic beer retailer Morgan Wolaver tells me that only one per cent of the land is given over to organic production.

The costs of farming, wholesaling and retailing will fall only when more organic produce is grown. Costs will also fall dramatically if Britain becomes less reliant on imports. As Geetie Singh and Esther Boulton point out, Britain is the biggest consumer of organic produce in Europe, yet is one of the smallest producers. Esther and Geetie have to import organic lettuces from Zimbabwe for their pub restaurants. As Geetie says, this is "absurd, as lettuces are the easiest of all vegetables to grow".

It is even more absurd that British brewers have to import organic hops from New Zealand, and also have to source some of their barley from abroad. But even if all Britain's organic foodstuffs are home-grown, the cost to the public will remain high as long as retailers "charge what the market will bear". It is a patent nonsense that a can of humble baked beans should cost 10 pence more in organic form than in conventional form. If the giant supermarkets that dominate food retailing in Britain consider that organic food is only for the well-heeled chattering classes they will continue to price it high regardless of the cost of production. This keeps it beyond the reach of people on lower incomes, the very people whose diets would be improved immeasurably if they were able to afford better-quality food.

There is another reason why organic food is more expensive than conventional food: agricultural subsidies. "Cheap food" is a myth. It is also a cruel joke on the environment, for that alleged cheapness has been achieved at huge cost, by flooding land with chemicals, and pumping animals with steroids and antibiotics.

There are grants for farmers under the Common Agricultural Policy, plus grants from the British government. There are even grants for not farming the land – the setaside policy that encourages farmers to stop growing fruit, vegetables and cereals as a result of Europe's notorious food mountains. While millions starve or eke out a miserable existence in many desperately poor Third World countries, and with famine endemic in parts of Africa, enormous warehouses in Europe stock mountains of grain that could feed the hungry. The previously quoted Jonathan Swift would have great sport with setaside and food mountains if he were writing today.

The subsidies do not come cheap. They are paid for by taxpayers. If the subsidies were removed, and the true price of the damage to the environment and the costs of cleaning it up were calculated, it is likely that conventional food would be more expensive than organic food. A study by the Centre for Environment and Society at the University of Essex estimates that the costs of damage to the environment and repairing that damage may be as much as £208 per hectare of land.

In 1996, British water companies spent more than £200 million cleaning chemicals, nitrates, pesticides and herbicides that had run from farmland into the water supply. There is also the unknown cost of the damage done to the environment and biodiversity by chemical pollution. The crisis in the National Health Service could be reduced to some extent if people working in agriculture and its associated industries did not contract cancer and other life-threatening illnesses as a result of daily contact with toxic chemicals.

The cost to the British taxpayer of the BSE crisis has been calculated conservatively at £4.5 billion. The final cost of the foot-and-mouth crisis will be far higher. The spokesmen for the National Farmers Union, a body largely dominated by the representatives of agribusiness, may weep, wail, rend their garments and hold out the begging bowl, but the crises are to a large extent are of their making.

Nature can wreak a terrible vengeance. Pumping animals full of steroids to increase their weight artificially, and turning herbivores into cannibals are unnatural practices that have inevitably reaped the whirlwind.

While fat cheques are written every year for farmers engaged in conventional farming, the pickings for converting to organic production are slim indeed. In England, the Organic Farming Scheme (OFS) gives some minimal support to farmers during the period when land must be allowed to lie fallow while it purges itself of chemicals. There are then payments (ranging from £450 a hectare for arable land to £350 for improved land, and £50 for unimproved land) for five years. These are supplemented by three annual lump-sum payments of £300, £200 and finally £100, which are mainly for certification costs with such bodies as the Soil Association. There are no further payments after five years. Similar schemes operate in Wales and Scotland. It's an improvement on past government indifference but is best described as small beer.

The worm turns

Suddenly, and excitingly, in the first few years of the new century, organic beer has turned from the monoculture of Caledonian's Golden Promise into a small but vibrant sector of the market. As this guide was being completed, Fuller's Brewery in West London announced that its organic Honey Dew beer would be available in draught cask-conditioned form in both the spring and autumn every year. A new version, with the addition of cranberry juice, was due to be launched in the summer of 2002. Honey Dew is now the brewery's second most successful brand after London Pride.

Maltsters, including such major companies as Crisps and Simpsons, are now able to supply domestically grown organic grain. Supplies are hit-and-miss, and brewers complain that the varieties of malt delivered to them can vary from batch to batch. This can cause problems, as yeast strains acclimatise to particular varieties of malt, and function less well if the variety changes. Other complaints centre on the quality of organic grain, but this will surely improve with experience, selectivity and regular production.

Brewers and maltsters have united to save the finest malting barley grown in Britain. Maris Otter had been delisted by large farmers and seed merchants on the grounds that it was not sufficiently high yielding, that is, did not produce as much per hectare as more modern varieties. Maris Otter is now grown by farmers strictly to contract by brewers willing to pay a premium. The juiciest, biscuity malting barley lives on, and small amounts are now being grown organically. In Scotland, the Caledonian Brewery is working with whisky distillers and farmers to develop regular supplies of organic Golden Promise barley.

On the hop front, there has been a small revolution. In spite of the best efforts of the government, whose unloved and unmissed Ministry of Agriculture withdrew funding from a hop research farm in Herefordshire, important work on hop development continues at Wye College in Kent. As I record in the section on hops, new varieties of low-climbing plants known as hedgerow hops have been a considerable success, and need fewer sprays than conventional tall-climbing varieties.

Several farms will grow organic hops in 2003, supplementing Peter Hall's organic Target in Kent. Not only will the cost of importing hops be reduced as home-grown varieties spread, but drinkers will also be faced by greater diversity where aroma and flavour are concerned. English hop growers can take pride in the fact that they have dramatically decreased the levels of chemicals used on hops, which is good for consumers and the environment. As I have been an organic thorn in their side for years, I unreservedly raise my glass and salute their willingness to listen to other views, and change their methods of husbandry.

There is even some good news on the cider front. While Bulmers, the *capo di tutti capi* of cider making, has withdrawn its first effort at an organic cider (packaged in a can: a very green concept, that) it has created new organic apple orchards in Herefordshire, and will allow smaller cider makers to buy those apples. A small toast to Bulmers ... but not in Strongbow.

On the negative side, it is significant that Britain's four national brewing groups are missing from this guide. Scottish Courage, Coors Brewing, Interbrew and Carlsberg-Tetley are all global giants. ScotCo is the only British-owned group of the four, but its biggest brand is the "French" lager Kronenbourg. The "Big Four" account for eight out of ten pints of beer brewed in Britain, and they cannot muster a single organic beer between them. They won't while they are wedded to a philosophy that puts volumes and profits ahead of consumer choice.

Nevertheless, there are grounds for optimism. Smaller producers are listening to consumers. Brewers no longer lag behind drinkers' demands, or dimiss those demands as a passing fad. Making organic beer and cider will deepen our pleasure and appreciation of these noble drinks. Of even greater importance, such production – dependent on craft and skill rather than spray cans – is a small contribution to a greener, cleaner and safer future. Drink organic, think organic, and let us live in harmony with nature.

Prosit!

Roger Protz
St Albans, April 2002

Chapter 1
Brewing Methods

Beer, whether ale or lager, is made by extracting the sugars from barley malt and other cereals, and fermenting the sweet liquid with yeast, which converts the sugars into alcohol.

Barley malt is the basic raw material – even "wheat beers" usually contain around 50 per cent barley malt. Most barley is grown for cattle feed, for non-alcoholic drinks and for confectionery. Brewers want only the finest varieties that give a juicy and biscuity character to beer, and which are low in nitrogen: too much nitrogen can cause a haze in the finished beer, and is another good reason for farming organically.

Barley begins its transition to malt in a maltings. It is washed or steeped in tanks filled and replenished with water for around 60 hours. Steeping not only washes the grain to remove dirt and other impurities from the fields, but also kills bacteria and wild yeasts that would impede germination and fermentation. The wet grain is laid out on the floors of the maltings and raked several times a day for four to five days as the grain starts to germinate.

Amazing biochemical changes take place inside the grain as it germinates: the starch in the grain becomes soluble, enabling it to be transformed into malt sugar. The obvious sign that germination is taking place is the rootlet breaking through the husk. The plant's embryo starts to grow, triggering a change that turns proteins into enzymes that will eventually transform starch into sugar in the brewery.

Only partial germination takes place: if the grain were allowed to germinate fully, it would start to consume its own sugars. This is the great skill of the maltster, to judge when germination has gone far enough. He does this by the simple, age-old method of chewing some grain. If it soft and friable in the mouth, then "modification" – the growth of the embryo and the solubility of the starch – has progressed successfully.

Germination is then stopped completely by heating the grain in kilns, large rooms with steeply pitched roofs. The floors are made of slotted metal, and the grain is shovelled on to the floors. Heat comes up from below, provided by fires that are usually created today by gas, the cleanest source of heat. The damp "green" malt stays in the kiln for 48 hours. Brewers want pale malt in large quantities, as it contains the highest proportion of natural enzymes.

The darker the malt, the lower the level of enzymes. Dark malt is produced by kilning the grain at a higher temperature. Such types of malt as brown, black and chocolate, as well as unmalted roasted barley that is widely used in stout brewing, have no soluble starch left to turn into sugar but are used for colour and flavour. They look similar to coffee beans and, in fact, are often used as a coffee substitute in cheaper instant coffees.

The malt is delivered to the brewery, where it is cleaned to remove any stones or nails that may have got through the malting process. It's then crushed or "cracked" in a mill. The mill has several settings: it can reduce the grain to flour, and this is blended with coarser grits and the husk of the grain. The husk is vital as it acts as a natural filter during the next stage of the process, and it's the husk that is one reason why barley is the preferred grain for brewers. Wheat, for example, doesn't have a husk and becomes soggy and mushy during the mashing process.

While the malt is being cracked, the brewing staff will check the quality of the "liquor", the brewing term for water. Ale brewers want hard water, rich in gypsum and magnesium, while lager brewers prefer soft water, low in salts. The house yeast strain will be checked in a laboratory to ensure it's pure and has not developed any dead or infected cells.

Ale brewing

In a classic ale brewery, the brewing process begins in a large round vessel known as the mash tun. It's usually built with copper, cast iron or stainless steel, and insulated with a wooden jacket. It has a lid made of two semi-circles of wood, raised by pulleys. Hot liquor and malt pour into the tun; pale malt may be augmented by such darker malts as crystal, amber, brown or chocolate, according to the recipe. The thick, porridge-like mixture stands in the tun for an hour or more while saccharification – the conversion of starch to sugar – takes place. The conversion is the result of work by enzymes in the malt. They produce maltose, a highly fermentable form of sugar, and dextrin, which cannot be fermented by conventional brewer's yeast but which gives roundness and body to the finished beer.

When the brewer is satisfied that starch conversion has taken place by running off samples from taps on the side of the mash tun, mashing is stopped by pumping in more hot liquor, which kills the enzymes. The slotted base of the tun is opened and the sugary extract, called wort, is run off to a holding vessel. To make sure that no sugars are left behind, the grain is then sprayed with more liquor to wash them out. Revolving arms in the roof of the tun sprinkle the grain: this is known as sparging. The used or spent grain is sold as cattle feed.

The wort is pumped to the copper (called the brew kettle in the United States). It may be made of copper, but more likely stainless steel in a modern brewery. It works on a similar principle to a coffee percolator. The wort, heated to boiling temperature, gushes up a central column and pours into the main body of the vessel.

Hops are added at the start of the boil, half way through, and then just before the boil ends after an hour or more. As many of the aromatic and bittering qualities of the hops are distilled off during the boil, the final addition, known as "late hopping", is vital to give a good hop character to the beer. The boiling wort extracts acids, tannins and oils from the plants.

At the same time, bacteria are killed along with any enzymes that have survived mashing and sparging. Some of the malt sugars will caramelise, to give body and colour to the beer. Depending on the recipe, special brewing sugars may also be added during the boil for both flavour and to encourage a good fermentation.

When the boil is finished, the hopped wort runs into a receiving vessel, where it cools. The used hops are not wasted: they are sold either as pig food or as compost for farmers and gardeners. As soon as the hopped wort is cool, it's pumped to fermenting vessels and thoroughly mixed with the house yeast strain. While fermenters can be enclosed, traditional ale brewers in Britain prefer open vessels that allow them to monitor the fermentation process.

Yeast is a fungus that feeds on sweet sugar. As it devours the maltose in the wort, the yeast recreates itself and builds a thick blanket on top of the liquid. The method is known as warm or top fermentation, a method that produces not only alcohol but rich, fruity characteristics as a result of the production of natural chemicals known as esters. So much yeast is produced by fermentation that some is kept back in the brewery for future use, while the remainder is sold to the food industry as yeast extract. In Britain, the best-known form of yeast extract is Marmite, whose factory is based in the major brewing town of Burton-on-Trent.

Ale brewers like to keep their beer in the fermenters for seven days or "two sabbaths". Fermentation ends when most of the sugars have turned to alcohol and carbon dioxide. Some sugar, in the form of maltose and dextrin, is desirable for roundness and palate. The beer, known as "green beer", is pumped to conditioning tanks, where it's left to stand for a few days to purge itself of rougher, unwanted alcohols and esters.

The beer now goes in different directions. It may be filtered and pasteurised, and run into either bottles or sealed containers called kegs. Keg draught beer has to be served with applied carbon dioxide, nitrogen or a mixture of both in the pub or bar.

The finest form of draught beer is cask conditioned, dubbed "real ale" in Britain. From the conditioning tanks, the beer is racked into pot-bellied casks with living yeast. Additional hops and brewing sugar may be added for aroma and to encourage a second fermentation in the cask. The casks are transported to pub cellars, where fermentation continues, adding maturity, flavour and more alcohol to the beer.

The casks have taps knocked into bung holes to serve the beer, and are also vented, with porous wooden pegs driven into smaller openings on top known as shives. This allows excess carbon dioxide to vent off. It's important that some gas is left behind, to give the beer its condition and sparkle. This is achieved after a day by replacing the soft peg with a harder one that stops gas escaping and oxygen entering the cask.

When the beer has "dropped bright", with yeast and protein dragged to the bottom of the cask by the action of finings, the beer is ready to be served. Plastic tubes or "lines" are attached to the tap and simple suction pumps operated by familiar handpumps draw the beer from cellar to bar. Bottled beer that contains live yeast is known as bottle conditioned or bottle fermented.

The finings used to clear cask beer come in the main in the form of isinglass, which is made from the bladders of fish, the sturgeon in particular. The use of isinglass presents a problem for vegetarians and vegans. As the sturgeon is being fished to the point of extinction as a result of demand for caviar, it is time the brewing industry researched other ways in which cask beer can be cleared of yeast. Such vegetable alternatives as Irish Moss should be considered. Most bottle-fermented beers are free from isinglass: the yeast falls naturally to the bottom of the containers.

Lager brewing

Lager comes from a German word meaning storage. It's similar to the English word larder, an old-fashioned cool area or room that pre-dates refrigeration. Attempts to brew beer in the summer and keep it cool had been tried for many centuries in central Europe, but the production of lager beer on a commercial scale was only possible with the invention of ice-making machines in the nineteenth century.

Classic lager brewing begins in mash kettles, where malt is mixed with brewing liquor. European malt traditionally is "less modified" than malts used in ale brewing. This means that the process that makes it possible to turn starch into sugar has not progressed as far in the maltings, so has to be completed during mashing. This is done by a more exhaustive mashing regime.

In the mash kettle, the temperature is raised to a level where protein in the grain begins to break down. A third of the mash is then pumped to a second kettle, where the temperature is increased so that saccharification can take place. The temperature is raised again to kill the enzymes, then that portion of the mash is returned to the first kettle. The second portion of the mash goes through the same procedure, but the final third remains in the original kettle, in order to give a degree of malty sweetness and fullness of palate to the beer.

This method of mashing is known as "decoction", whereas ale mashing is called infusion. At the end of the long mashing cycle, the grain is clarified in yet another vessel called a lauter tun, which has a slotted base. The wort is then pumped to coppers or brew kettles and boiled with hops. As with ale brewing, the hopped wort is cooled and run into fermenting vessels, and thoroughly mixed with yeast.

Primary fermentation is slower as a result of lower temperatures, and may last for ten days. At the end of primary fermentation, the beer is pumped to lager tanks in the cellars of the brewery, where the beer is stored or lagered at just a degree or two above freezing point.

Unfermented sugary wort may be added to encourage a second fermentation. This fermentation is slow, and may take several weeks or months. The classic Czech lager, Budweiser Budvar, is lagered for three months. Some strong lager beers, such as German Bocks, enjoy up to nine months in the lager cellar.

This slow fermentation produces a high level of natural carbon dioxide, while the yeast slowly falls to the bottom of the tanks. This gives rise to the term "bottom fermentation" to describe the method, though cold fermentation is more correct, as ale yeast also falls to the bottom of fermenters when it is overcome by the alcohol it has produced. Cold fermentation purges most of the fruity esters found in ale, and the finished result is a clean and quenching beer.

With the rise of global brewers, there is intense pressure to speed up lager fermentation, and stop the costly business of storing heavily taxed liquid for several months. American Budweiser is lagered for around 21 days, for example, while South African Breweries, which now owns the Velké Popovice brewery in the Czech Republic, has cut lagering time from 60 to 30 days.

When the lagering period is finished, the beer is usually filtered and often pasteurised, though craft brewers prefer to avoid pasteurisation, which gives a cooked and cardboard note to delicate lager beers. In Germany and the Czech Republic, draught lagers are usually served by means of their own natural carbonation, not by applied gas.

Chapter 2
Hops

New Zealand Hallertauer is a superb hop variety with a delightful floral, piny and resiny aroma and flavour, with some delicious hints of citrus fruit. But one of the many pleasures of beer drinking comes from the careful blend of different hops that gives individual brews their distinctive signatures. If beer after beer uses just New Zealand Hallertauer, they can become rather samey and lacking in distinctiveness.

The reason why so many of the British-brewed organic beers in this guide use the New Zealand hop is not hard to divine. At present there is only one regular grower of organic hops in England, and his annual crop is bought well in advance by just a handful of brewers.

Other brewers, anxious to make organic beer, have to go abroad for their hops. There are organic hops grown in Germany, but most of those are snapped up for domestic use. One Belgian hop farmer is making an organic interpretation of the English Golding. But far and away the biggest supply of hops grown without the use of fertilisers, herbicides and pesticides comes from New Zealand in the form of Hallertauer and Pacific Gem. It is one of the curiosities of modern brewing that a hop that started life in the

Hallertau region of Bavaria, and migrated to New Zealand, now makes the long trip to the British Isles.

New Zealand has an almost identical climate to that of the British Isles. The reason it's possible to grow organic hops in the South Pacific with comparative ease is that the region is isolated from the rest of the world. The pests and diseases that make the farming of hops difficult in many other countries have not so far affected New Zealand – or Australia, for that matter. In particular, the damson hop aphid, a pest that can munch its way through a hop garden at frightening speed, is unknown Down Under.

Mindful of the fact that pests and disease are now prevalent in the Pacific North-west hop-growing areas of the United States, Australia and New Zealand maintain a strict quarantine to keep their countries free of similar problems. Other plants, herbs and fruit would be threatened if aphids, mildew and wilt broke through the Antipodean defences.

The major hop-growing regions of England – Kent, Herefordshire and Worcestershire – suffer from every imaginable problem. As well as aphids, red spider mites also enjoy a hearty lunch on the hop plant. Powdery mildew, downy mildew and wilt turn bines – the stems on which the plants grow – black and rotten. The traditional response of English hop farmers has been to reach for the spray can and a cocktail of chemicals.

Modern thinking believes that such an approach does more harm than good. It not only covers plants in chemicals, but also destroys the natural habitat where such predators as ladybirds, hoverfly larvae, lacewings and parasitic wasps live, and from where they can launch attacks on pests. Nature can do the job best.

Important work on growing hops with less reliance on chemicals was carried out at the ADAS Rosemaund research farm at Preston Wynne in Herefordshire. When I visited the farm in the late 1990s I found areas of hop cultivation where grass and weeds were allowed to grow between the hop bines, providing a perfect habitat for predators. On the same site, new varieties of "dwarf hops", that grow to only half the height of conventional ones, had been developed. They were being harvested by specially adapted tractors that cut down two rows or "curtains" of hops in one operation, and were less labour-intensive as a result. The new types of hop – now called "hedgerow" – needed much lower levels of pesticides and herbicides.

But ADAS Rosemaund had its grants from the Ministry of Agriculture withdrawn. Its scientists were told to go and work on commercial farms, where a different philosophy prevails. It seemed that the development of hops that needed fewer sprays and fully organic hops had received a major and possibly terminal setback.

When I visited the lonely outpost of organic hop production in Kent, I found a farmer bursting with enthusiasm, and a passionate belief in avoiding harmful chemicals. Peter Hall at Marden grows organic Target. He also growns conventional hops, but he says his organic Target taste better

Hop types

Conventional hops will continue to be grown in abundance as a result of the globalisation of brewing. The cone of the hop plant has a yellow powder called lupulin that contains the oils and bittering compounds needed by the brewer. The compounds include the alpha acids that give bitterness to beer.

Hops divide into two main categories: bittering hops and aroma hops. Craft brewers will often blend both varieties – such as the Fuggle and the Golding – in their beers, but big global brewers are more and more switching to "high alpha" hops for bitterness. International lager brands and keg ales are served so cold and covered in applied gas that delicate aroma hops have little or no impact. The United States leads the way in growing high alpha varieties, followed by Germany, England, Australia and China.

High alpha hops are so important globally that they are bought and sold on the world commodity market. There is enormous pressure on hop farmers to concentrate on this lucrative sector of the market. While there is good news about the development of low-spray and organic hops in England, it would be naive to think that the future is sound for aroma hops. If we were to lose aroma hops, beers would cease to have the characteristics that make beer drinking such a delight.

as they are free from chemicals. His organic variety is more expensive as it is labour-intensive, but the cost accounts for only a fraction of the price of a pint of beer.

Peter Hall's list of the chemicals used by conventional hop growers makes depressing reading: nitrates, organo-phosphorous compounds, weed killers and fungicides. In place of chemicals, he ploughs in legumes that provide natural nitrogen to the soil, and eventually turn into green manure. The legumes also preserve nutrients in the soil. Later in the season, he sows white mustard seed around and between the trellises where the hop bines grow. The seed produces more green manure, and provides a habitat for lacewings and ladybirds. He also sprays the tops of the bines with a solution of soapy water that kills aphids.

Peter tackles mildew, which can turn hops black, by "rogueing" – digging out infected bines – and spraying with copper oxychloride, the only fungicide approved by the Soil Assocation (though this is currently being reviewed by the European Union). Every February, he ploughs in "shoddy" – waste from the clothing industry that is rich in nitrogen – which feeds the roots of the bines, and conditions the soil.

Farmer Hall is no longer a lone figure. ADAS Rosemaund has gone, but Hop Research International at Wye College in Kent has continued the vital work of developing new hop varieties that are less prone to attack by pests and disease, and which therefore need fewer chemical sprays. Wye College, part of Imperial College in London, works with the Hop Industry Board to monitor new varieties. Dr Peter Darby at HRI Wye is at pains to point out that new varieties are developed by classic cross-breeding – that is, taking the best genes from existing breeds to grow new ones. There are no genetically modified hops.

In 2001, HRI Wye submitted two new varieties for European Plant Variety Rights recognition. Pilgrim is a conventional tall-climbing variety similar to Wye Target, but with a greater resistance to wilt and downy mildew. Pilot is a new hedgerow variety. At the same time, a further hedgerow variety combining for the first time resistance to the fungal pathogens that cause wilt and mildew, and also to the damson hop aphid, has been developed for organic production, with trials taking place on two farms.

Dr Darby says that the small crop from the 2001 harvest produced a "pleasing brew" from a regional brewer. This was a trial beer, not made for commercial sale. Trial brews using new hop varieties are also made for HRI Wye by the pilot brewery at Brewing Research International in Surrey, and by the Craft Brewing Association, which can make small batches of beer.

In 2003, three hop farms registered as organic will start to grow hops. They will be joined by a fourth farm awaiting registration. An organic version of First Gold will be grown in Worcestershire, while in Sussex organic versions of Whitbread Golding Variety (a tall-climbing variety) and a hedgerow hop will be grown. HRI Wye is also developing a new hedgerow hop, codenamed S26, that has "outstanding resistance to wilt disease".

Dr Darby says that the key to developing new hops that need either low chemical assistance or which can be grown organically is resistance to the damson hop aphid.

"It's the most difficult to control. The pest literally explodes across a hop

Medicinal hops

Hops have an important role to play in preventing illness. Scientific studies have shown that the constituents of hops, including humulone and lupulone, act as anti-carcinogens and anti-oxidants. These have a beneficial effect on the whole cardiovascular system, as well as on bones and the brain.

Research at HRI Wye in Kent indicates that one of the most promising of the hop compounds is xanthohumol. Results from the 2001 hop season showed that the proportion of xanthohumol in the resins can be increased dramatically by selective breeding in new varieties.

In Germany, the brewing faculty at the University of Weihenstephan, near Munich, is working closely with local hospitals to research into the ways in which hops can be used in the fight against cancer.

garden before the predators arrive. The best resistance to the hop aphid has to be hedgerow hops. They grow on low trellises, and that tips the balance in favour of the predators."

He adds that hedgerow hops are the varieties of the future because they are more controllable and economic as they need fewer pesticides. Organic varieties, of course, will require no pesticides at all. Dr Darby also says that successful hedgerow varieties must have good bitterness, flavour and yield, but the potential already lies in existing varieties. What is needed is successful breeding of new ones.

English hop farmers can take pride in the fact that they lead the world in developing hedgerow hops, and now have the lowest use of chemical sprays of any country outside Australasia. Existing hedgerow varieties have reduced chemical treatments by up to 50 per cent. Dr Darby hopes that, within the next eight years, further hop varieties incorporating aphid resistance would be bred at HRI Wye that could reduce pesticide applications by up to 90 per cent of traditional use. The lower use of chemicals is not only important for hop growing; it means a massive reduction in "chemical drift", whereby sprays are carried on the breeze to neighbouring areas.

The development of organic hops will mean a "massive investment", Dr Darby points out.

"It's like running the London Marathon. Dedicated enthusiasts can do it, but amateurs find it difficult."

Now the enthusiasts – traditional hop farmers – have the wind at their back and the finishing line in sight. Thanks to genuine consumer demand, organic beers will be made at an even faster rate as English-grown hops are produced on a wider scale.

The lights are on green.

Chapter 3

Organic Beers of Great Britain and Ireland

For most of the 1990s, organic beer in Britain was confined to one lonely product, Golden Promise from the Caledonian Brewery in Edinburgh. Other brewers said that, as organic beer was such a niche market, it was adequately filled by that one product and no one else need bother. Brewers also muttered darkly about the near impossibility of obtaining organic malt and hops, and the poor quality of the materials when they could be found.

But then consumers found their voice and voted with their wallets. Organic beer was no longer confined to specialist shops. It lost its "beards-and-sandals" image as supermarket shelves emptied as soon as organic produce appeared. By the end of the decade and the dawn of a new and greener millennium, the organic food and drink sector was worth £1 billion a year and was growing by 40 per cent a year. Golden Promise suddenly faced competition. A tiny trickle became a small flood as more and more brewers

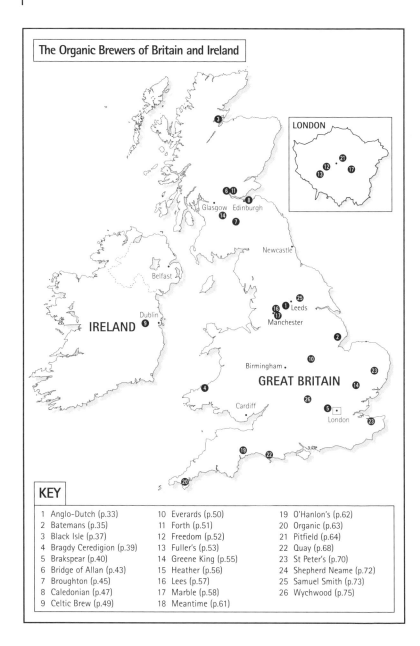

The Organic Brewers of Britain and Ireland

LONDON

Glasgow
Edinburgh
Newcastle
Belfast
Dublin
IRELAND
Leeds
Manchester
Birmingham
GREAT BRITAIN
Cardiff
London

KEY

1 Anglo-Dutch (p.33)	10 Everards (p.50)	19 O'Hanlon's (p.62)
2 Batemans (p.35)	11 Forth (p.51)	20 Organic (p.63)
3 Black Isle (p.37)	12 Freedom (p.52)	21 Pitfield (p.64)
4 Bragdy Ceredigion (p.39)	13 Fuller's (p.53)	22 Quay (p.68)
5 Brakspear (p.40)	14 Greene King (p.55)	23 St Peter's (p.70)
6 Bridge of Allan (p.43)	15 Heather (p.56)	24 Shepherd Neame (p.72)
7 Broughton (p.45)	16 Lees (p.57)	25 Samuel Smith (p.73)
8 Caledonian (p.47)	17 Marble (p.58)	26 Wychwood (p.75)
9 Celtic Brew (p.49)	18 Meantime (p.61)	

hurried to meet a genuine and often passionate demand for organic beer. Three pubs in London appeared, selling only organic beer, wine and food.

The major maltsters, such as Crisps and Simpsons, began to supply organic malt, removing the need to get supplies from mainland Europe. The hop farmers no longer produced bell, book and candle when the dread word "organic" was muttered nervously in their presence. The success of new varieties of hedgerow hops, which grow to only half the height of conventional varieties and are less prone to pests and disease, prompted further research. Within a few years it is possible that organic hops will be grown in sufficient amounts in England to offer both brewers and drinkers more choice than just New Zealand varieties. The demand for organic beer has been met by dedicated regional and smaller craft breweries. The national brewers, whose dedication is to volumes and profits, are conspicuous by their absence.

ANGLO-DUTCH

Anglo-Dutch Brewery, Unit 12, Savile Bridge Mills, Mill Street East, Dewsbury, West Yorkshire WF13 6QQ. Tel 01924 457772.

Mike Field (Anglo) and Paul Klos (Dutch) opened their brewery in November 2000 and soon added four organic beers to the range of cask-conditioned ales. Mike also runs the buffet bar at Dewsbury railway station, where the beers are on sale. They are also occasionally available at the famous Stalybridge railway station buffet: the station is on the Manchester to Huddersfield line and the buffet is one of the last surviving examples of the Victorian style in the country. It has won a "Best Refurbishment" category in the annual awards for pubs organised by English Heritage and the Campaign for Real Ale (see *Britain's 500 Best Pubs*, published by Carlton Books, 2000).

Whitterus Organicus (3.8% ABV)

Ingredients: lager malt. New Zealand Hallertauer and Hersbrucker hops.

Spikus Organicus (4.2% ABV)

Ingredients: pale malt, lager malt. New Zealand Hallertauer and Hersbrucker hops.

Whitterus Supreme Ale (WSA) (4.3% ABV)

Ingredients: pale malt, lager malt. New Zealand Hallertauer and Hersbrucker hops.

Ghoulis Organicus (4.5% ABV)

Ingredients: pale malt, lager malt. New Zealand Hallertauer and Hersbrucker hops.

Tasting note: the beers are available on draught only from spring to autumn. The main hop is Hallertauer; Hersbrucker is used as a "late hop" at the end of the copper boil. The beers were not available for tasting when the guide was being compiled.

Availability: draught cask-conditioned. A bottling line is being installed.

BATEMANS

George Bateman & Son Ltd, Salem Bridge Brewery,
Wainfleet All Saints, Lincolnshire PE24 4JE.
Tel 01754 880317. Fax 01754 880939.
Email **enquiries@bateman.co.uk** Website **www.bateman.co.uk**

Bateman is a much-loved, family-owned brewery in an idyllic setting on the banks of the River Steeping. An ivy-covered and armless windmill, which used to grind the malt for the brewery, rises like a welcoming sentinel from the flat Lincolnshire countryside. Batemans started life in 1874 as a farmers' brewery: local farmers supplied grain and, in return, were sold ale for their families and labourers. The founder, George Bateman, was the grandfather of the current chairman, also named George. The company has retained deep roots in the local community. During the economic depression between the two world wars of the 20th century, George Bateman's father had to sack some of his workers. When he saw them standing around on street corners in Wainfleet, he immediately hired them again.

Although Bateman's beers can be found throughout the country, the company devotes much time, energy and investment to its 70-strong estate of pubs, which are a careful and sensitive blend of traditional values and modern comfort. The rural, family-owned charm of the brewery was ruptured in the 1980s when some of the Batemans decided to sell their shares and retire on the proceeds. The only way to save the brewery was for George Bateman to raise the cash to buy out his relatives. With the active support of his wife, Pat, daughter Jaclyn and son Stuart, George stumped the country, visiting banks and financial institutions, until he finally got the financial backing he needed.

Since then, Batemans – using its time-honoured slogan of "Good Honest Ales" – has gone from strength to strength, winning the prized Champion Beer of Britain award from CAMRA for its XXXB bitter and a clutch of other awards. A visitor centre opened in 2000 and a new brewhouse, which will allow production to increase, was brought on stream in March 2002.

The name Yella Belly recalls a more bucolic time when Lincolnshire folk who picked mustard seed in the fields were nicknamed "Yella Bellies" as a result of the stains on their clothes. The Yella Bellies quaffed large quantities of ale to slake their thirsts. In the rural economy of the 19th and early 20th centuries, the ale they drank would have been made from ingredients free from agri-chemicals.

Head brewer Martin Cullimore uses two suppliers for his organic malt. The varieties vary depending on which grains are available. He has been using either Alliot or Schooner, malting barleys previously unknown not only to the writer but to Martin himself. His hops come from New Zealand, but he is working with a hop grower in the English Midlands to develop regular supplies of organic First Gold, a "hedgerow" variety that grows to only half the height of conventional hops. They will take a couple of years to become available as the land has to go through a period of conversion to remove chemical residues. Yella Belly was first introduced as a seasonal beer but was an instant success and is now a regular brew.

Yella Belly Organic Bitter (4.2% ABV)

Ingredients: pale malt. New Zealand Pacific Gem hops.

Tasting note: golden colour with a rich creamy malt and pear drop fruit aroma. Tart, spicy hops dominate the palate, balanced by biscuity malt. The finish is intensely bitter and hoppy, with a quinine-like note, the bitterness offset by citrus fruit and juicy malt.

Availability: draught cask-conditioned and bottled.

BLACK ISLE

Black Isle Brewery, Old Allangrange, Munlochy, Ross-shire IV8 8NZ, Scotland. Tel 01463 811871. Fax 01463 811875.
Email **djg@blackislebrewery.com** Website **www.blackislebrewery.com**

Black Isle, launched in 1998, is a small independent brewery in the Scottish Highlands. A five-barrel plant is based in converted farm buildings by an 18th-century house near Inverness. The area has a long tradition of providing some of the finest malting barley in Scotland: Allangrange comes from the Gaelic Allan-Chrain, which means "fertile field of corn". Cask beers are sold locally, while bottled beers are distributed throughout Scotland and can also be bought from an on-site shop. Black Isle owns one pub, the late 17th-century Plough Inn at Rosemarkie. It plans to concentrate production on organic beer: at present its two cask-conditioned ales, Red Kite and Yellowhammer, are not organic.

Goldeneye Organic India Pale Ale (4% ABV)

Ingredients: pale ale malt, crystal malt and wheat malt. Goldings, German Hersbrucker and New Zealand Hallertauer hops.

Tasting note: golden/amber ale with a pronounced aroma of grapefruit from the hops, nutty malt, citrus fruit and tart hops in the mouth, with a long finish balanced between grapefruit, malt and hops; it finally becomes dry and bitter. Wonderfully refreshing beer.

Availability: draught keg and bottled.

Wheat Beer (4.5% ABV)

Ingredients: pale ale malt and wheat, with lemon peel and coriander. German Hersbrucker and New Zealand Hallertauer hops.

Tasting note: a cloudy wheat beer with a tempting aroma of lemon peel and coriander, zesty and quenching in the mouth, with a lingering finish dominated by citrus and spice.

Availability: draught keg and bottled.

Scotch Ale (4.5% ABV)

Ingredients: pale ale malt, dark crystal malt and wheat. Goldings and New Zealand Hallertauer hops.

Tasting note: chestnut-coloured beer with a nutty and dark grain aroma, rich, chewy malt in the mouth balanced by tangy hops, with hops coming through in the finish, balancing the dark, roasty grain and almost vinous fruit. A fine example of a traditional Scotch. Unfiltered beer with live yeast.

Availability: bottle-fermented.

Thornbush Porter (4.5% ABV)

Ingredients: pale ale malt, wheat, chocolate malt, crystal malt and oats. New Zealand Hallertauer hops.

Tasting note: a dark ruby-coloured beer with a bitter and roasted malt aroma, hedgerow fruits and floral hops in the mouth balancing rich malt and creamy oats, and a big finish in which bitter hops, roasted grain, creamy oats and dark fruit vie for attention.

Availability: bottled.

Stout (4.5% ABV)

Ingredients: pale ale malt, wheat, chocolate malt, crystal malt and oats. New Zealand Hallertauer hops.

Tasting note: red/black beer, with roasted grain and a hint of orange fruit on the aroma, a firm malty palate with creamy oats and hops, and a long finish with dark fruit, roasted malt and bitter hops. Mellow and smooth.

Availability: draught keg and bottled.

Blond (4.5% ABV)

Ingredients: lager malt, pale ale malt and wheat. German Hersbrucker and New Zealand Hallertauer hops.

Tasting note: a lager-style beer, pale gold in colour, with a biscuity malt and grassy hop aroma, juicy malt and tart hops in the mouth, and a lingering bitter-sweet finish with a fine balance of malt and hops.

Availability: draught keg and bottled.

BRAGDY CEREDIGION

Bragdy Ceredigion Brewery, Brynderwen, Llangranog, Llandysul, Ceredigion SA44 6AD, Wales. Tel 01239 654099. Fax 01239 654099. Email **brian@ceredigionbrewery.fs.business.co.uk**

Brian and Julia Tilby set up their craft brewery in 1997 in a converted barn on Wervil Grange Farm in the coastal area of West Wales. The full mash, five-barrel plant produces cask-conditioned and bottle-fermented beers from floor-malted Maris Otter barley and Challenger, First Gold, Hallertauer and Fuggles hops. No chemical additives are used and the bottled beers are suitable for vegetarians. The organic beer Blodeuwedd was launched in 2000. The name comes from the Welsh legend of Blodeuwedd, a beautiful maiden created from flowers by two powerful magicians. She plotted with her lover to kill her husband and, as punishment, was turned into an owl. Blodeuwedd is the Welsh for "flower face". The striking label was designed by Julia Tilby.

Blodeuwedd (4.5% ABV)

Ingredients: organic pale malt and Hallertauer hops. Primed with organic sugar for secondary fermentation.

Tasting note: golden colour with a citrus hop and juicy malt aroma. Peppery hops dominate the palate, balanced by creamy malt, while the finish is hoppy and bitter with a continuing citrus fruit note.

Availability: draught cask-conditioned and bottle-fermented.

BRAKSPEAR

W H Brakspear & Sons PLC, The Brewery, New Street, Henley-on-Thames, Oxon RG9 2BU. Tel 01491 570200. Fax 01491 410254. Email **frontoffice@brakspear.co.uk** Website **www.brakspear.co.uk**

Brakspear is one of Britain's oldest breweries. Brewing has been taking place on the site close to the Thames since at least 1700. The Brakspear family is distantly related to Nicholas Breakspear, the only English Pope. In 1799, Robert Brakspear went into partnership with Richard Hayward to run the brewery in Henley. It was Robert's son, William Henry, who gave his name to the company, and expanded it with great enthusiasm, buying pubs in the

Thames Valley and selling his ales as far away as London: boats would take beer to London and return laden with malt and hops.

The Victorian brewery and offices are dominated by an arched entrance and an imposing chimney. The brewhouse has fine mash tuns and coppers, but the most interesting feature is the rare "dropping system" of fermentation. Two banks of open-topped fermenters are ranged on two storeys. Fermentation begins in the top vessels, and after a few days the bottoms of the vats are opened, and liquid and yeast drop to the vessels below. The system aerates the wort and leaves dead yeast cells and unwanted protein behind. Fermentation continues with increased vigour for several more days, encouraged by Brakspear's multi-strain house yeast that attacks malt sugars with great tenacity. Brakspear has taken up the organic torch with great enthusiasm and now has four beers made with natural, unsprayed ingredients. It won the organic beer competition staged by the Society of Independent Brewers (SIBA) in 2000 and 2001. The winners are given a national listing by supermarket group Safeway.

Head brewer Peter Scholey uses whatever organic malt varieties are available. He has used a German variety called Scarlet but that is not always available. The beers use the same materials, with the exception of lager malt in Naturale, but the percentages vary. A Belgian version of the famous Kent Golding hop is specially contract-grown for the brewery. The classic Golding is the variety known as East Kent: head brewer Peter Scholey jokes that his Belgian variety is the "East of Kent Golding". He stresses that while the four bottled beers have the same strength they are all separate brews.

Ted & Ben's Organic Beer (4.6% ABV)

Ingredients: pale ale malt, crystal malt. Belgian Goldings, English Target and German Hallertauer aroma hops.
Tasting note: copper-coloured beer with a pronounced floral hop aroma balanced by juicy malt and spice notes. A good

balance of malt, hops and spices in the mouth, with a long, lingering finish in which bitter hops begin to dominate but are well balanced by biscuity malt and hints of citrus fruit. Brakspear's first organic beer was brewed in draught form in 2000 and was so successful that a bottle-fermented version followed. It's named after the brewery's security officer and sales manager, who were asked to think of a name for the new beer. In the end it seemed simpler to use their names. The beer was the runner-up in the ale category of the 2001 SIBA competition.

Availability: draught cask-conditioned and bottle-fermented.

Live Organic (4.6% ABV bottled; 4.2% ABV draught)

Ingredients: pale ale malt and crystal malt. Belgian Goldings, English Target and German Hallertauer aroma hops.

Tasting note: pale amber/copper colour. Pronounced cobnuts aroma balanced by biscuity malt. Tart citrus orange palate with bitter, spicy hops. Long finish dominated by increasingly dry and bitter hop character, with tart fruit, spices and creamy malt. Target is the dominant hop in this beer. Overall champion 2000 and 2001 SIBA competition.

Availability: bottle-fermented.

Naturale (4.6% ABV)

Ingredients: lager malt and crystal malt. Belgian Goldings, English Target and German Hallertauer aroma hops.

Tasting note: pale bronze colour. Rich creamy malt aroma with a good underpinning of spicy hops. Malt dominates the palate with a gentle balance of hops. The finish starts malty but becomes dry and assertively hoppy. Naturale won first prize in the lager category of the 2001 SIBA competition. It's not a true lager made by cold

fermentation, but it is fermented at a lower temperature than other Brakspear ales. Peter Scholey says that one strain in his remarkable house yeast is tolerant of low temperature.
Availability: bottled.

Organic Beer (4.6% ABV)

Brewed exclusively for Vintage Roots distribution company.
Ingredients: pale ale malt and crystal malt. Belgian Goldings, English Target and German Hallertauer aroma hops.
Tasting note: bronze beer with a big peppery/spicy hop aroma. Juicy malt and spicy hops dominate the mouth, with a long bitter, biscuity malt and spicy hop finish. An outstanding beer with a wonderfully quenching character bursting with complex hop aroma and flavours.
Availability: bottled.
NB The bottled versions of the Brakspear beers are not fined with isinglass and are therefore suitable for vegetarians and vegans.

BRIDGE OF ALLAN

Bridge of Allan Brewery Ltd, The Brewhouse, Queens Lane, Bridge of Allan, Stirlingshire FK9 4NY, Scotland. Tel 01786 834555. Fax 01786 833426.
Email **brewery@bridgeofallan.co.uk** Website **www.bridgeofallan.co.uk**

The brewery was founded in 1997 by Douglas Ross, who is committed to making hand-crafted beers using the finest natural ingredients. He says that making good beer is as time-consuming and demanding as good wine. Bridge of Allan, known as the Gateway to the Highlands, is an attractive Victorian spa town on the banks of the River Allan, and close to the Wallace Monument and Stirling Castle. The area once boasted 32 breweries as a result of fine soil that grew top-quality barley, plus pure water from the Ochil Hills.

Ben Nevis 80/- Ale (4% ABV)

Ingredients: Maris Otter pale malt, crystal malt, amber malt, dark roast malt, wheat. Hallertauer Hersbrucker hops for bitterness, Hallertauer hops for aroma.

Tasting note: deep copper colour, with a biscuity, roasted malt aroma with strong hints of sultana fruit. There are spicy, peppery hops in the mouth balanced by dark grain. A refreshing finish has a good balance of tart fruit, roasted grain and gentle hop bitterness. Ben Nevis is Scotland's highest mountain at 4,406 feet, with peaks often covered in snow and shrouded in mist. The beer named in its honour is called an 80-shilling ale, a traditional Scottish "heavy". The name comes from a Victorian practice in Scotland of invoicing beer according to strength, with a range of 60, 70, 80 and 90 shilling ales. Such beers are typically rich in malt character but relatively lightly hopped by English standards.

Availability: draught cask-conditioned and bottled.

Glencoe Wild Oat Stout (4.5% ABV)

Ingredients: Maris Otter pale malt, crystal malt, amber malt, dark roast malt, chocolate malt, oats and wheat. Hallertauer Hersbrucker hops for bitterness, Hallertauer for aroma.

Tasting note: black with a ruby edge and barley white head. Ravishing aroma of burnt and roasted malt with hints of cappuccino coffee and raisins. Bitter dark fruit, creamy oats and spicy hops dominate the mouth, while the massive finish has roasted malt, oats, spicy hops and sour fruit. It finally becomes intensely bitter. The oats grow wild in the Forth Valley. The

stout is as dark and mysterious as the glen itself, the scene of the dreadful massacre in 1692 when the Campbell and MacDonald clans clashed. Glencoe is part of the West Highland Way, a 95-mile walk from Glasgow to Fort William through the beauty of the Lowlands and the Highlands.
Availability: draught cask-conditioned and bottled.

Lomond Gold Blonde Ale (5% ABV)

Ingredients: Maris Otter pale malt, crystal malt, amber malt, dark roast malt, wheat. Hallertauer Hersbrucker hops for bitterness, Hallertauer hops for aroma.

Tasting note: pale bronze beer with a fruity, pear-like aroma, followed by spicy hops and citrus fruit in the mouth. The finish is bitter-sweet, with creamy malt balanced by spicy hops. It finally becomes dry and bitter. Loch Lomond and the surrounding area are known as the Trossachs and form Scotland's first National Park. Loch Lomond is the country's biggest loch or lake, and is on the West Highland Way.

Availability: draught cask-conditioned and bottled.

NB The beers are approved by the Vegetarian Society. A gift pack of all three beers is available from the brewery.

BROUGHTON

Broughton Ales Ltd, Broughton, Peebles-shire ML12 6HQ, Scotland. Tel 01899 830345. Fax 01899 830474.

Email **beer@broughtonales.co.uk**   Website **www.broughton-ales.co.uk**

Broughton is one of Scotland's oldest "new wave" small independent breweries. It was founded in 1979 by David Younger, a member of the famous Scottish brewing clan that, with the McEwans, created the giant Scottish & Newcastle group. Broughton was built on a smaller scale in a single-storey building overlooking fields with grazing sheep, the blue-green Borders hills rising in the background. Broughton is best known as the birthplace of John Buchan, the adventure writer: one of the brewery's beers, Greenmantle Ale, is named after one of Buchan's Richard Hannay stories. There is a small Buchan museum in the town. The brewery was bought in 1995 by Giles Litchfield, owner of the Whim Brewery in Derbyshire, who expanded the range of beer and now sells half its production in bottled form. It supplies around 200 outlets in Scotland and has a sizeable export market in North America.

Border Gold (6% ABV bottled; 4.2% ABV draught)

Ingredients: pale ale malt (variety varies according to availability). New Zealand Hallertauer and Pacific Gem hops.
Tasting note: a hoppy nose dominated by floral Hallertauer character and citrus fruit leads to a firm malty palate balanced by spicy hops and citrus fruit. The long finish is exceptionally dry, hoppy and bitter by Scottish standards: the bottled version has 35 units of bitterness.
Availability: draught cask-conditioned spring and autumn; bottled.
The bottled versions of the beers are sold predominantly in Scotland but are also distributed in England by Booths supermarkets, John Lewis Partnership, Vinceramos and Vintage Roots.

Waitrose Organic Ale (4.6% ABV)

Brewed exclusively for the Waitrose supermarket group.
Ingredients: pale ale malt (variety varies according to availability). New Zealand Hallertauer and Pacific Gem hops.
This beer is identical to bottled Border Gold (see above) but is brewed to a lower strength and less bitterness – 25 to 30 units bitterness.
Availability: bottled.

Angel Organic Lager (5% ABV)

Ingredients: lager malt (variety varies according to availability). New Zealand Hallertauer hops.

Tasting note: a golden beer with a rich creamy malt aroma and floral hops, quenching malt in the mouth balanced by spicy hops, and a long finish that starts bitter-sweet and malty, and finishes dry and bitter.

Availability: bottled.

CALEDONIAN

Caledonian Brewing Co Ltd, 42 Slateford Road, Edinburgh, EH11 1PH. Tel: 0131 337 1286. Fax 0131 313 2370.
Email **info@caledonian-brewery.co.uk**
Website **www.caledonian-brewery.co.uk**

(See Heroes of Organic Beer.) Golden Promise, Britain's first regularly-brewed organic beer, takes its name from Golden Promise, Scotland's finest variety of malting barley. In fact, it's no longer used, as Caledonian – known in Scotland as "the Caley" – cannot obtain sufficient quantities of the organic version. However, the brewery has gone into partnership with a group of Scottish farmers to grow more organic Golden Promise, and hopes to restore the variety to the beer when supplies become available. It has also dropped English Target hops from Kent in favour of New Zealand Hallertauer, as supplies from Kent are not sufficiently reliable.

Golden Promise (5% ABV bottled, 4.4% ABV draught)

Ingredients: 100% Optic pale ale malt. New Zealand Hallertauer hops.

Tasting note: a golden beer, as the name implies, with a rich Ovaltine/ biscuity malt aroma balanced by spicy hops. The biscuity and hoppy palate has background notes of cinnamon and vanilla, and the finish is quenching, with rich malt, intense hop bitterness and a pronounced hint of that tangy childhood confectionery, sherbet lemons. It has 18–20 units of colour and 50–52 units of bitterness.

Availability: the bottled version is distributed throughout Britain and is in most major supermarkets. The cask version also has wide distribution.

Organic Lager (5% ABV)

Brewed exclusively for Tesco.

Ingredients: 100% Optic pale malt. New Zealand Hallertauer hops.

Tasting note: pale gold beer with a sweetcorn, biscuity malt and lemon fruit aroma, citrus fruit, floral hops and rich malt in the mouth, followed by a lingering finish with lemon fruit, tart hops and mellow malt. An excellent British effort at a European lager.

Availability: bottled.

Organic Premium Ale (5% ABV)

Brewed exclusively for the Co-op.

Ingredients: 100% Optic pale malt. New Zealand Hallertauer hops.

Tasting note: a golden beer with a mellow, biscuity malt aroma balanced by light floral hops and a hint of vanilla. Juicy malt and tart, spicy hops dominate the mouth, while the finish starts bitter-sweet but becomes dry and hoppy with hints of tangy citrus fruits.

Availability: bottled.

Organic Beer (5% ABV)

Brewed exclusively for Tesco.

Ingredients: 100% Optic pale malt. New Zealand Hallertauer hops.

Tasting note: golden ale with a big malty aroma balanced by spicy hops and pear-like fruit, followed by a firm malty palate underscored by tart hops, and a finish that becomes increasingly bitter and hoppy, with citrus fruit and biscuity malt notes.

Availability: bottled.

NB All four beers use the same raw materials, but they are blended differently, as the aromas and flavours indicate. Organic brewing sugar is used in the lager.

CELTIC BREW

Celtic Brew, Enfield, Co Meath, Eire. Tel 00353 404 41558.
Email **craftbrew@premierbeers.ie**   Website **www.premierbeers.ie**

Celtic Brew, opened in 1997 by the then Irish Prime Minister John Bruton, is a fast-growing, state-of-the-art craft brewery based on the site of a sixth-century monastery founded by St Finian of Clonard. The monastery survived until the 12th century, and for a time was second only in importance to Rome.

Finian (also spelt Finnian) followed in the footsteps of St Patrick: he not only helped spread Christianity in Ireland but also developed the country's brewing culture. Brewing artefacts and implements discovered in the remains of the monastery suggest the site not only had its own brewery but was also a school of brewing, making it the first formal centre for brewing education in Ireland and possibly the whole of the British Isles. The artefacts are now on view at Clonmacnoise, another ancient monastery founded with St Finian's help.

Celtic Brew quickly outgrew its initial capacity and has had to install a new brewhouse, going from a ten hectolitre brew-run to 30 hectolitres. It has doubled its output every year since 1997.

The beers are now available throughout Ireland, and exported to mainland Britain, Finland, France, Germany, Iceland, Italy and Australia.

As well as organic lager, Celtic also brews stout and an Irish Red Ale, the oldest indigenous beer style in Ireland. It predates the porters and stouts of the 18th century by several hundred years.

St Finian's Organic Lager (5% ABV)

Ingredients: pale Pilsner malt. New Zealand Hallertauer hops.

Tasting note: pale gold beer with a dense head of foam. Classic European Pilsner aroma of fresh corn and slightly toasted malt, with juicy malt in the mouth balanced by floral hops, and a lingering finish balanced between malt and hops, with a delicate touch of lemon fruit.

Availability: bottled and draught.

EVERARDS

Everards Brewery Ltd, Castle Acres, Narborough, Leicester LE9 5BY. Tel 0116 201 4100. Fax 0116 281 4199.

Email **mail@everards.co.uk** Website **www.everards.co.uk**

Everards is a family-owned brewery with deep roots in the East Midlands: its flagship beer, Tiger Best Bitter, underscores long-standing support for the

Leicester Tigers Rugby Union club. The brewery celebrated its 150th anniversary in 1999, and the present chairman, Richard Everard, is the great-great grandson of the founder. The brewery owns 154 pubs in Leicestershire and surrounding areas, and also supplies around 500 free trade pubs with its beer. Terra Firma was first brewed in 2002 and will initially be available only on draught for the spring period.

Terra Firma (4.5% ABV)

Ingredients: Chariot pale malt, crystal malt (88% pale, 12% crystal). Belgian Goldings hops.

Tasting note: a polished deep copper coloured beer with a big Goldings hop resin aroma balanced by nutty crystal malt. There are bitter hops and tart fruit in the mouth, followed by a long finish with roasted malt, tart fruit and bitter, spicy hops. The unusually large proportion of crystal malt gives the beer its luscious colour and a pronounced nutty aroma and flavour. The beer has 50 units of colour and 37 units of bitterness.

Availability: cask-conditioned, springtime.

FORTH

Forth Brewery Co Ltd, Eglinton, Kelliebank, Alloa FK10 1NU, Scotland. Tel 01259 725511. Fax 01259 725522

Alloa, with such famous names as Calder and Younger, once vied with Edinburgh for the title of Brewing Capital of Scotland, its success built on the brilliant quality of the local water. One by one the breweries closed, and it seemed that Alloa would become a brewing desert when Maclays, the last independent in the town, closed its doors in 1999. But several members of the Maclay's management opened a new, small plant on the outskirts of the town. As well as its organic beer, it produces three cask-conditioned ales. Its beers are distributed by Belhaven, Caledonian, the Beer Seller, and Flying Firkin

Saaz Organic Lager (4.1% ABV)

Ingredients: pale lager malt. Hallertauer and Saaz hops.

Tasting note: a golden beer with a complex aroma of toasted grain, sweetcorn, floral hops and hints of lemon fruit. Juicy malt and spicy hops dominate the palate, while the finish is refreshing, with tart fruit, creamy malt and bitter hops.

FREEDOM

Freedom Brewing Company, 11 Galena Road, Hammersmith, London W6 OLT. Tel 020 8748 0903.

Email **info@freedombrew.com**   Website **www.freedombrew.com**

Freedom opened in 1995 in Fulham as the first dedicated lager micro-brewery in Britain, under the tutelage of brewmaster Alastair Hook (see Meantime). Freedom outgrew the site, and now has two brew-restaurants in London, but at present the organic version of its Pilsner lager – renamed "Organic Beer" in 2002 – is brewed under licence by a German brewer: Freedom will not name the brewery but says it has considerable experience in the organic field. The beer is brought to Britain in tankers and bottled by the Hepworth Beer Station Brewery in Horsham, West Sussex. Freedom hopes to bring brewing back to Britain as soon as a suitable brewer can be found who can give a true Pilsner character to the beer. With a nice touch

of irony, Freedom's office address in Hammersmith is named after a hop variety, Galena. The beer is supplied in draught form to three dedicated organic pubs in London: the Crown in Hackney, the Duke of Cambridge in Islington, and the Pelican in Ladbroke Grove.

Freedom Organic Beer (4.8% ABV)

Ingredients: Pilsner lager malt. Hallertauer hop varieties.

Tasting note: biscuity, slightly toasted malt aroma with floral hops, quenching malt and delicate hops in the mouth, followed by a juicy, malt-dominated finish balanced by floral hop notes.

Availability: draught keg and bottled.

FULLER'S

Fuller Smith & Turner plc, Griffin Brewery, Chiswick Lane South, Chiswick, London W4 2QB. Tel 020 8996 2000. Fax 020 8995 0230.
Email **fullers@fullers.co.uk** Website **www.fullers.co.uk**

Fuller's is one of Britain's best-known and most successful family-owned regional brewers. In the 1990s and early part of the new century, it shrugged off an overall decline in beer sales, especially in the cask ale sector, and grew its own brands by phenomenal amounts. London Pride is now one of the best-known and leading cask beers in the country, while the super premium ESB (Extra Special Bitter) is another market leader. The Griffin Brewery, in a picturesque setting alongside the Thames, has been on the site for more than 350 years. Messrs Fuller, Smith and Turner formed their partnership in 1845 and descendants of the families are still involved in running the company.

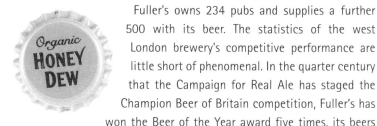

Fuller's owns 234 pubs and supplies a further 500 with its beer. The statistics of the west London brewery's competitive performance are little short of phenomenal. In the quarter century that the Campaign for Real Ale has staged the Champion Beer of Britain competition, Fuller's has won the Beer of the Year award five times, its beers have been "best in class" no fewer than nine times, and ESB has been voted Best Strong Ale an unprecedented seven times. Honey Dew was first brewed using conventional materials. Sales soared when it was converted to organic materials and it's now the fastest-growing organic beer in the country. Trials were conducted with several types of organic honey

(which is added during the copper boil with hops): the type that gave the best flavour and reacted well with the other ingredients and, in particular, Fuller's house yeast, came from Argentina. As the sugar in the honey is attacked by the yeast and converted to alcohol, the finished beer is not cloyingly sweet.

Organic Honey Dew
(5% ABV bottled; 4.3% ABV draught)
Ingredients: Chariot or Optic pale malt, organic honey. English Target hops.
Tasting note: pale bronze beer with a delightful rich honey aroma. Juicy malt and spicy hops come through in the mouth, while the finish is a pleasing balance of ripe malt, bitter hops and dry honey.
Availability: draught cask-conditioned and bottled.

GREENE KING

Greene King plc, Abbot House, Westgate Brewery, Westgate Street, Bury St Edmunds, Suffolk IP33 1QT. Tel 01284 763222. Fax 01284 706502.

Website **www.greeneking.com**

Greene King has transformed itself from a large regional company based in East Anglia into a "super-regional" as a result of the takeover and closure of Morland of Abingdon and Ruddles of Rutland. It owns 1,600 pubs in the South-east, including a substantial number in the Thames Valley, and also supplies some 3,500 other outlets. Further acquisitions cannot be ruled out, and a merger with the country's other super-regional, Wolverhampton & Dudley, has been rumoured. The company was founded in 1799 by Benjamin Greene. Frederick King opened a rival brewery on Westgate Street in 1868, and the two companies merged in 1887.

The Greene family has included the great novelist Graham Greene (who would occasionally visit Bury to start the mash for a special brew, including one to mark his 80th birthday), and Sir Hugh Greene, a famously liberal Director-General of the BBC, who went on to become chairman of the brewery. A brewery museum opened in 2001 and it includes a new oak vat that stores a strong ale called 5X, which is blended with a weaker beer to form Strong Suffolk Ale, the last remaining example of a style known as Country Ale, which in the 18th and 19th centuries was stored in wooden vats for several years. The museum is open Monday–Saturday and Sundays in summer (01284 714382).

Ruddles Organic (5.1% ABV)

Ingredients: pale and crystal malts from Crisps of Suffolk. German Spalter hops.

Tasting note: pale copper colour with a rich malt and slightly toasted grain aroma, with sultana fruit and tangy hops in the mouth, followed by a long finish with fruit, toasted grain and peppery hops.

Availability: bottled. Widely available in major supermarkets. In 2001 the beer was available draught cask-conditioned in the autumn and may appear in that form again.

HEATHER

Heather Ale Ltd, Craigmill Brewery, Craigmill, Strathaven, Lanarkshire ML10 6PB, Scotland. Tel 01357 529529. Fax 01357 522256.
Email **fraoch@heatherale.co.uk** Website **www.heatherale.co.uk**

Heather Ale is one of the most fascinating and innovative breweries in Britain. It was founded by Bruce Williams in 1992 and sprang to fame with Fraoch, based on an ancient Scottish recipe that uses flowering heather as well as conventional grains and hops (the heather contains its own wild yeasts that encourage fermentation). Bruce has since added a Grozet Ale made with gooseberries and Ebulum brewed with the addition of elderberries. The seaweed for Kelpie is collected from the beach at Arisaig, just south of Mallaig, on the west coast of Scotland: the pickers have fine views of the islands of Eigg, Rum and Skye. The seaweed is added at the rate of eight kilos to the mash in the brewery. Bruce says the seaweed acts as a clearing agent and he doesn't have to add isinglass finings (made from fish bladders) at the end of the brewing process. This means the beer is suitable for vegans and vegetarians. He hopes to convert all his beers to organic ingredients.

Kelpie Organic Seaweed Ale (4.4% ABV)

Ingredients: pale and crystal malts from Simpsons, seaweed. New Zealand Pacific Gem hops.

Tasting note: rich iodine and ozone aromas from the seaweed, with nutty malt, floral hops and tart, herbal flavours in the mouth, followed by a long, intensely bitter and refreshing finish with iron-like flavours from the seaweed balancing rich malt and hops.

Availability: draught cask-conditioned and bottled.

LEES

J W Lees & Co (Brewers) Ltd, Greengate Brewery, Middleton Junction, Manchester M24 2AX. Tel 0161 643 2487.
Fax 0161 655 3731.
Website **jwlees.co.uk**

When the brewery was founded by John Willie Lees in 1828, Middleton Junction was a rural area. Now it's part of the urban sprawl between Manchester and Oldham. But the brewery, with its tall and slightly wonky chimney, and splendidly traditional brewing vessels, remains true to craft brewing. It even employs its own coopers to build and repair wooden casks. Lees owns 175 pubs, all of which serve cask-conditioned ale. Half of that production is still in wooden casks.

Lees brews mild and bitter but is best known for its remarkable strong ales, Moonraker (7.5% ABV), and the 11.5% Harvest Ale, brewed every autumn and released just before Christmas. The company's entry into the organic market is a lager brewed exclusively for a small group of pubs and clubs in the North-west owned by Paul Heathcote.

Heathcote's Organic Lager (5% ABV)

Ingredients: Scottish malt. New Zealand hops.

Tasting note: Polished gold colour, with a rich malt aroma with hints of toffee and perfumy hops, tart and spicy hops in the mouth balancing juicy malt, and a full-bodied finish dominated by rich malt and gently bitter hops.

MARBLE

Marble Brewery, 73 Rochdale Road, Manchester M4 4HY.
Tel/fax 0161 610 1073.
Email **vance@marblebeers.co.uk** Website **www.marblebeers.co.uk**

Owner Vance de Bechevel transferred his small, five-barrel plant at the back of the Marble pub to organic production in 2000 when a number of health food shops and off-licences in Manchester asked for beers made without pesticides and fertilisers. Brewer James Campbell produces 12 barrels of beer a week and has to grind his own malt – most small craft brewers buy malt ready ground – as the Soil Association won't allow organic malt to pass through mills that also grind

conventional grain. The magnificent pub was built in 1888 by a local and long-defunct brewery called McKenna. It has glazed brick walls, mosaic floors and a barrelled ceiling. The pub food is as good as the beer. Customers are warned that the beers have a slight protein haze as they are not fined with isinglass, but this does not deter the large numbers that pack the pub.

N/4 Bitter (3.8% ABV)

Ingredients: pale, crystal and wheat malt, with coriander (10gms per 900 litres). New Zealand Hallertauer hops.

Tasting note: pale amber beer with citrus fruits, coriander and rich grain on the aroma, a hoppy, spicy and fruity palate, followed by a finish that is balanced between creamy malt and tart hops, and finally becomes dry.

Availability: draught cask-conditioned.

Cloudy Marble (4% ABV)

Ingredients: pale, crystal and wheat malts. New Zealand Hallertauer hops.

Tasting note: amber-coloured beer with a pronounced floral hop and citrus fruit aroma, tart fruit, hops and juicy malt in the mouth, and a big, quenching finish dominated by bitter hops and malt.

Availability: draught cask-conditioned.

Manchester Bitter (4.2% ABV)

Ingredients: pale, lager and wheat malts. German Hersbrucker and New Zealand Hallertauer hops, dry hopped in cask with Hersbrucker and New Zealand Pacific Gem.

Tasting note: a pale gold beer with a big hoppy and fruity aroma, the fruit reminiscent of melons. Sweet malt in the mouth is balanced by tart hops and citrus fruit, while the long finish becomes dry and bitter but with a good malt and fruit balance.

Uncut Amber (4.7% ABV)

Ingredients: pale, crystal, chocolate and wheat malts. New Zealand Hallertauer hops, dry hopped in cask with New Zealand Pacific Gem.

Tasting note: russet-coloured beer with a rich malt, tart fruit and chocolate aroma. Chocolate, malt and fruit dominate the palate, while the finish is bitter-sweet, with notes of roasted grain, chocolate and hops.

Availability: draught cask-conditioned.

Old Lag (5% ABV)

Ingredients: pale, lager and crystal malts. German Hersbrucker and New Zealand Hallertauer hops.

Tasting note: pale copper colour, with hop resins dominating the aroma, tart hops and juicy malt in the mouth, and a long finish balanced between rich malt, bitter hops and citrus fruit.

Availability: draught cask-conditioned.

Chocolate Heavy (5.5% ABV)

Ingredients: pale, crystal and chocolate malts. New Zealand Hallertauer hops.

Tasting note: ruby-black beer with a vinous and chocolatey aroma, rich chocolate, burnt grain and bitter hops in the mouth, and a roasted grain finish balanced by a vinous, port wine character, but balanced by tart hop notes.

Availability: draught cask-conditioned; seasonal

MEANTIME

Meantime Brewing Co, 2 Penhall Road, Greenwich, London SE7 8RX.
Tel 020 8293 1111.
Email sales@mean-time.co.uk   Website www.mean-time.co.uk

Meantime is a rarity in the world of brewing: it doesn't want people to know about the existence of the company. The aim is to brew bespoke beers for specialist customers, such as London bars, restaurants, quality pubs (it owns one itself: the Greenwich Union in Royal Hill, Greenwich) and supermarkets with a genuine passion for good beers and a willingness to market them.

The brewery is like Dr Who's Tardis: it's tucked away on a bleak industrial estate in South-east London, but once through the doors you find yourself in a substantial brewhouse with superb vessels imported from the best mainland European manufacturers.

The inspiration for Meantime is brewmaster Alastair Hook, a British brewer who trained at both Heriot-Watt School of Brewing and distilling in Edinburgh, and at the world-renowned Weihenstephan University in Munich. His passion is for the classic European styles, and at Meantime he has created such beers as a Kolsch-style warm-fermented golden ale based on the style developed in Cologne, a Vienna "Red" lager, using large amounts of well-cured Munich and Vienna malts, and a true Bavarian-style wheat beer, booming with bubble gum aromas and flavours.

In Britain, Alastair ran the Pack Horse brewery and night-club in Ashford, Kent, before accepting the challenge of running the brewery at Oliver Peyton's Mash & Air brew-restaurant in Manchester. Alastair brewed a range of beers that carefully complemented the dishes on offer. From Manchester, he moved to London to set up a similar operation for Peyton's Mash brew-restaurant in Great Portland Street. He continues to brew some of Mash's beers at Meantime: the brewery is handily just over the road from Charlton Athletic Football Club, of which Alastair is a passionate supporter.

For non-British readers, the name of Meantime is a subtle play on the fact that the Meridian line at Greenwich is used to plot international time zones, and the zero degrees of Greenwich is known as Greenwich Meantime.

Meridian Organic Lager (4.7% ABV)

Brewed exclusively for Sainsbury's supermarkets.

Ingredients: Pilsner malt, caramalt and Munich malt. Hallertauer hop varieties from Germany and New Zealand.

Tasting note: Amber-gold beer with an enticing aroma of slightly toasted grain, cornflour and tart hops. Juicy malt, lightly bitter hops and a touch of citrus fruit dominate the palate, with a finish finely balanced between hop bitterness and creamy malt.

Availability: bottled.

O'HANLON'S

O'Hanlon's Brewing Company Ltd, Great Barton Farm, Whimple, Devon EX5 2NY. Tel 01404 822412. Fax 01404 833700.
Website **www.ohanlons.co.uk**

British pubgoers are used to fake "Oirish" pubs on every high street and they could be forgiven for thinking that an Irish brewery on a farm in Devon has more than a touch of the Blarney about it. But it's the real McCoy. John O'Hanlon, a large, genial, rugby-playing Irishman, opened a brewery in Vauxhall, south London, in 1996 to supply his pub, called O'Hanlon's, in Clerkenwell. Beer lovers attended in vast numbers to quaff such brilliant and genuine Irish beers as Red Ale, Dry Stout and a Port Stout brewed with the addition of port: the latter is a famous Dublin cure for a hangover dispensed by barmen known rather alarmingly as curators.

In 2000 John and his wife Liz moved the brewery – lock, stock and unloaded barrels – to Devon, where they continue to brew the full range of beers for O'Hanlon's in London (now under new ownership) as well as other free-trade accounts. The rye in John's organic beer is not malted as an organic version is not available. He uses an unmalted rye similar, he says to flaked barley: the grain is steamed until it swells, and is then passed through heated rollers. The starch in the grain is gelatinised, making it open to attack by the enzymes in the pale and other malted grains in the mash tun.

Organic Rye Beer (5% ABV)

Ingredients: pale malt (70%), crystal malt (10%), rye (20%). New Zealand Hallertauer hops.

Tasting note: pale copper colour with a pronounced rye bread aroma and a touch of tart fruit. Dark grain, bitter hops and juicy malt dominate the palate, while the finish becomes intensely bitter, with an iodine-like note, and a bready grain character, balanced by sharp fruit.

Availability: bottled; sold nationwide in Safeway and in specialist beer shops.

ORGANIC

Organic Brewhouse, Unit 1, Higher Bochym Rural Workshops, Cury Cross Lanes, near Mullion, Helston, Cornwall TR12 7AZ.
Tel 01326 241555. Email **a.hamer@btclick.com**

A brewery that wears its heart on its sleeve. Andy Hamer opened his plant in 2000, overlooking Goonhilly Downs and its famous radio masts. Andy uses his own source of natural mineral water, and his brewing equipment is arranged as a mini "tower system", a much-favoured Victorian system whereby water, grain, mashing, boiling and fermentation are arranged one above the other, and flow naturally by gravity without the need for pumps. The two beers are available to pubs and retail outlets in Cornwall and occasionally head north through wholesalers.

Lizard Point (4% ABV)

Ingredients: pale malt, crystal malt (4%). New Zealand Hallertauer hops.

Tasting note: golden beer with a rich, hoppy aroma, followed by juicy malt, hops, and apple and pear fruit in the mouth, and a dry, malty finish balanced by good hop bitterness.

Availability: draught cask-conditioned and bottle-fermented

Serpentine Dark Ale (4.5% ABV)

Ingredients: pale malt, crystal malt, chocolate malt and wheat malt. New Zealand Hallertauer hops.

Tasting note: a ruby-red beer with a booming aroma of roasted grain, chocolate and floral hops, with rich malt and chocolate flavours dominating the mouth, and roasted grain, chocolate and bitter hops in the long finish.

PITFIELD

Pitfield Brewery, the London Beer Company Ltd, 14 Pitfield Street, Hoxton, London N1 6EY. Tel 020 7739 3701.

Website **www.pitfieldbeershop.co.uk**

(See also Heroes of Organics). Martin Kemp's Pitfield Brewery stands alongside the Beer Shop, which has won international acclaim as one of the finest retailers of quality ales and lagers, including a large number of organic beers. All the Pitfield beers are brewed with organic materials and are available in bottle-fermented form and draught cask-conditioned on demand. The brewery is highly flexible and can produce batches as small as just 70 bottles.

The beers are conditioned in cask for between two and three weeks before being racked into bottle or cask. The beers are reseeded with yeast and maltose syrup to encourage secondary fermentation. Bottles are stored in the brewery for a further two weeks before being released. No finings are added to either cask or bottle, so the beers are suitable for vegans and vegetarians; they may contain a natural haze.

As well as the regular brews, Martin also produces occasional one-off organic specials, such as a Pumpkin Porter for Halloween and Valentine Ale in February. The beers are on sale in London's three pubs devoted to organic food and drink: the Crown in Victoria Park, Hackney, the Duke of Cambridge in Islington, and the Pelican in Ladbroke Grove. Martin brews a house beer for the organic pubs called singhboulton named after the owners, Geetie Singh and Esther Boulton. The beers are available in mixed cases of 12 bottles by mail order from the Beer Shop.

Organic Lager (3.7% ABV)
Ingredients: Maris Otter pale malt. New Zealand Hallertauer hops
Tasting note: golden beer with a rich malt and spicy hop aroma, with rich creamy malt in the mouth balanced by tart hops. The finish has a big spicy, peppery hop presence, balanced by juicy malt.
Availability: keg and bottled.

Original Bitter (3.7% ABV)
Ingredients: Maris Otter pale malt, crystal malt and wheat malt. Challenger,

East Kent Goldings and Fuggles hops.

Tasting note: deep gold ale with a massive blast of hop resins on the nose: a very English hop aroma. Rich, nutty malt, dark fruits and bitter hops dominate the mouth, while the long finish becomes extremely dry and hoppy, balanced by creamy, nutty malt and bitter fruit.

Availability: draught cask-conditioned and bottle-fermented.

Shoreditch Stout (4% ABV)

Ingredients: Maris Otter pale malt, roasted barley, flaked barley. Challenger, Fuggles and Target hops.

Tasting note: a dark ruby beer with a smoky and roasted grain aroma balanced by tart hops. The palate is dominated by a sour and lactic note from the dark grain, with hints of liquorice and vanilla. The finish is long, with creamy malt, dark and bitter fruits, roasted notes and spicy hops. A superb beer that won the Society of Independent Brewers' award for Champion Speciality Beer in 2001.

Availability: draught cask-conditioned and bottle-fermented.

East Kent Goldings (4.2% ABV)

Ingredients: Maris Otter pale malt, crystal malt, wheat malt, flaked maize. East Kent Goldings hops.

Tasting note: amber-coloured beer with an aroma dominated by a big waft of resiny and spicy Goldings. Tart, spicy hops, citrus fruit and juicy malt combine in the mouth, followed by a finish with hop resins, creamy malt and bitter fruit. Goldings hops are grown throughout Kent but the East Kent variety is considered the classic. Like grapes, hops flourish in good soil – in the case of Kent, that generally means a well-watered loamy soil. Incidentally, those areas of Kent considered to be poor for hop growing are known as "Bastard Kent".

Availability: draught cask-conditioned and bottle-fermented.

Eco Warrior (4.5% ABV)

Ingredients: Chariot pale malt, brewing sugar. New Zealand Hallertauer hops.

Tasting note: hazy gold beer with an enticing aroma of juicy malt, perfumy hops and fresh-mown grass. Floral hops and rich grain dominate the palate, while the long finish is balanced between creamy malt, gently bitter hops and a touch of citrus fruit. The malts and hops give this beer a distinctly different aroma and flavour to the rest of the Pitfield range.

Availability: draught cask-conditioned and bottle-fermented.

Hoxton Best Bitter (4.8% ABV)

Ingredients: Maris Otter pale malt, crystal malt, dried malt, roast barley. Challenger, East Kent Goldings and Northdown hops.

Tasting note: copper-red beer with a rich roasted grain and resiny hop aroma, with a strong hint of chocolate in the mouth, balanced by roasted malt and tart hops. The finish has some citrus hop notes but is overwhelmingly malty and roasty. The beer was first called Hoxton Heavy as it was modelled on the Scottish style. Hoxton is the area where the brewery is located.

Availability: draught cask-conditioned and bottle-fermented.

Black Eagle (5% ABV)

Ingredients: Maris Otter pale malt, crystal malt, black malt, wheat malt. Challenger, Fuggles and Styrian Goldings hops.

Tasting note: dark russet beer with an aroma of hedgerow fruits and toasted grain. The palate is fruity, bitter but balanced by creamy malt, while the finish has a lingering juicy malt, tart fruit and bitter hops character. The beer is similar to a beer called Dark Star, a prize-wining ale brewed at Pitfield in the 1980s.

Availability: draught cask-conditioned and bottle-fermented.

QUAY

Quay Brewery, Lapin Noir Ltd, Brewers Quay, Hope Square,
Weymouth, Dorset DT4 8TR. Tel/fax 01305 777515.
Website **www.quaybrewery.com**

The Quay micro-brewery is housed in a fascinating complex in the
Weymouth harbour area of the town that includes brewing equipment from
a former larger commercial company, and an animated Timewalk exhibition
that enables visitors – children in particular – to learn the history of the
town, from its smuggling days, through the Regency period when Mad King
George and his court turned Weymouth from a fishing village into a major
seaside resort, to the modern days.

Hope Square, alongside the harbour, has wells that supplied copious
amounts of fine water, ideal for brewing. Three breweries once operated in
Hope Square, which also had a maltings: fine barley was grown in the
surrounding fields. The two biggest breweries stood cheek-by-jowl: they
were called Devenish and Groves. Devenish in its day was a giant of the
West Country, owning more than 400 pubs, with a second brewery in
Redruth, Cornwall. Devenish and Groves were fierce rivals until they merged
in the 1960s. The combined brewery finally closed in 1986, and the Groves
part of the building still stands, with its fine mash tuns, coppers and
fermenters on view.

Quay Brewery is run by Giles Smeath, who was a lawyer and a keen
Rugby Union player. In the finest traditions of the oval ball game, he enjoyed
a pint or three. He'd never brewed in his life when he took the plunge and
opened Quay in 1996. He learnt the brewing skills with Steve Wellington, a
master brewer who runs the Museum Brewery within the Bass Museum in
Burton-on-Trent. After a lot of reading and practising, Giles can talk to
Steve on almost equal terms, and he uses the famous Bass two-strain yeast
to produce his ales. With a two-strain yeast, the strains work at different

times and different temperatures to convert malt sugars into alcohol. Giles told me he put the Bass strain under a microscope and removed the smaller of the strains as he would have preferred to ferment with just one strain. After the first brew with the new yeast strain, he put it back under the microscope and found that the strain he'd removed had mysteriously reappeared. No wonder, before the age of Pasteur and microscopes, that brewers called yeast "God-is-Good".

Around 100 outlets take the beers in cask form. They are also bottled with their yeast in attractively old-fashioned pot-stoppered containers similar to those used for Grolsch lager. The bottled beers are on sale in bars within the Brewers Quay complex. Organic Gold began life as a "pantomime beer": Weymouth stages pantomimes every Christmas season and Giles has brewed Puss in Boots, Wizard of Oz, and Jack and the Beanstalk for the theatre bars. Jack and the Beanstalk was the prototype for Organic Gold.

Organic Gold (4.8% ABV)

Ingredients: pale malt. New Zealand Hallertau hops.

Tasting note: copper-coloured beer with a dense fluffy head. The aroma is rich and fruity – a fruitiness reminiscent of tart blood oranges. Fruit continues to dominate the palate, which is balanced by gently bitter hops. Citrus fruit lingers on into the finish, which becomes dry and bitter with a good hop presence.

Availability: draught cask-conditioned and bottle-fermented.

ST PETER'S

St Peter's Brewery Co plc, St Peter's Hall, St Peter's South Elmham, Bungay, Suffolk NR35 1NQ. Tel 01986 782322. Fax 01986 782505. Email beers@stpetersbrewery.co.uk Website www.stpetersbrewery.co.uk

St Peter's has one of the finest settings of any British brewery, behind a moated Tudor farmhouse that stands proud from the flat East Anglian countryside. The farm dates from 1280 and the moat was dug as a defence against marauding Vikings. Its present facade and fittings are the result of the dissolution of nearby Flixton Priory by Cardinal Wolsey, an act that prompted Henry VIII to embark on the wholesale closure of abbeys and monasteries in the 16th century to fill his coffers with much-needed gold and treasure. The exterior of St Peter's Hall is built of Caen stone from Normandy, and has a great chimney, lattice windows, and a large porched entrance with a tombstone. Inside, the Great Hall has a raftered ceiling, a 15th-century tapestry depicting Manna from Heaven, and a carved Madonna and Child. A second room, used for dining, includes a portrait of St Peter showing the old Basilica of St Peter's in Rome.

The importance of the site for brewing is an ancient borehole in the grounds that taps into an aquifer 300 feet below, which supplies a constant supply of fine water, ideal for brewing and miraculously (perhaps due to the influence of St Peter) free from modern agri-chemicals. The brewery was opened in 1996 by John Murphy, a marketing expert who advises companies on how to improve their images. On his travels, he was disappointed by the lack of British beer abroad, and decided to show others how to do it by running his own brewery. The modern plant is based in former dairy buildings and produces a wide range of beers, available on draught and in bottle. The company has achieved prominence due to the flagon shape of its bottles. They are based on an 18th-century flagon found by Mr Murphy in a shop in Gibbstown near Philadelphia. It was designed by an innkeeper named Thomas Gerrard who sold ale alongside the River Delaware.

Bottled versions of St Peter's beers are sold in supermarkets throughout Britain, in mainland Europe, and in Australasia, the Far East, Scandinavia and North America. The brewery owns a couple of pubs, including the Jerusalem Tavern in London (55 Britton Street, EC1), a careful recreation of an old London inn based in a former 18th-century coffee house. The brewery has a shop, and both brewery and hall are open for visits, while the hall can be booked for meetings and functions.

Organic Best Bitter (4.1% ABV)

Ingredients: Scottish Regina pale malt and crystal malt from Simpsons. New Zealand Hallertauer hops.

Tasting note: pale bronze beer with biscuity malt aroma balanced by peppery hops, an explosion of spicy, bitter hops on the tongue balanced by juicy malt, and a long finish dominated by iodine-like bitterness with a good underpinning of malt.

Availability: draught cask-conditioned and bottled.

Organic Ale (4.5% ABV)

Ingredients: Scottish Regina malt from Simpsons. New Zealand Hallertauer hops.

Tasting note: golden ale with a sweet malt and woody/resiny hop aroma, tart hops and sweet malt in the mouth, followed by a gentle but lingering finish balanced between juicy malt and tart but not over-bitter hops. Wonderfully refreshing.

Availability: draught cask-conditioned and bottled.

SHEPHERD NEAME

Shepherd Neame Ltd, 17 Court Street, Faversham, Kent ME13 7AX.
Tel 01795 532206. Fax 01795 538907.
Email **company@shepherd-neame.co.uk**
Website **www.shepherd-neame.co.uk**

Based in the heart of the Kentish hop fields, Shepherd Neame is the oldest brewery in the country and celebrated 300 years of continuous brewing in 1998. While brewing officially started on the site in 1698, records show that beer-making has been going on there since at least the 12th century.

The Faversham brewery was founded by a Captain Richard Marsh, and passed into the hands of a maltster named Samuel Shepherd, who was later joined by a hop-farming family, the Neames. The Neames still run the company today, with chairman Robert, vice-chairman Stuart and managing director Jonathan. While they have expanded the business by including such lagers as Hurlimann, Kingfisher and Oranjeboom, ale is the bedrock of the company, with such marvellously hoppy beers as Master Brew, Spitfire and Bishop's Finger.

The same water source is still used today, steam engines are on site and can be used in an emergency, and two teak mash tuns date from 1910. A visitors' reception area is based in a restored medieval hall. In 2000, Shepherd Neame invested £2.2 million in a new brewhouse that boosted production to 200,000 barrels a year. The company owns 390 pubs in the South-east of England and also supplies a further 500 outlets.

It has the pick of the finest Goldings and Target hops from the surrounding fields but currently has to source organic varieties from abroad. Shepherd Neame, close to the Channel Ports, has been at the forefront of a campaign to get the British government to reduce duty on British beer in an attempt to stem the flow of cheap imports from France and Belgium. It has been unsuccessful so far, even though the company was represented at a court hearing in Strasbourg by Cherie Booth QC, wife of Prime Minister Tony Blair.

Whitstable Bay Organic Ale (4.5% ABV)

Ingredients: English pale ale malt. New Zealand Gem and Hallertauer hops.
Tasting note: golden beer with a rich malt and pear-drop fruitiness on the nose, bitter hops, tart fruit and biscuity malt in the mouth, and a deep hoppy and bitter finish with sharp fruit notes.
Availability: bottled.

SAMUEL SMITH

Samuel Smith Old Brewery (Tadcaster), High Street, Tadcaster, North Yorkshire LS24 9SB.
Tel 01937 832225. Fax 01937 834673.

Samuel Smith is a proudly independent family-owned brewery, the oldest in Yorkshire, dating from 1758. There are two Smith brewing families in Tadcaster (known as the "Burton of the North" as a result of the fine quality of the brewing water there). A dispute within the family at the turn of the 20th century led to John Smith walking up the road and building his own site. John Smith eventually became part of Courage, which in turn now forms the Scottish Courage group, Britain's biggest brewer.

While John Smith is all high-tech brewing in modern vessels, Sam Smith ferments its beers in Yorkshire Squares, two-storey vessels made from slate. Fermentation starts in the lower chamber, and yeast and liquid rise through a porthole into the top one: fermenting beer returns through pipes to the bottom chamber, but the yeast is held back by a raised rim round the porthole. It is an old, simple but effective way of cleansing beer of yeast. Malt, hops, yeast and water combine to give the finished beers a rich fruitiness, while the reaction of fermentation in slate vessels gives rise to a high level of carbonation and the famous thick head of foam demanded by Yorkshire drinkers.

Water comes from a well on site and the beers are made without cereal adjuncts: in the 1990s, Sam Smith phased out the use of brewing sugar in order to concentrate on all-malt beers. Its Old Brewery Bitter is delivered in wooden casks to pubs, and coopers are still employed to make and repair casks.

The company owns more than 200 pubs. Its two dark bottled beers, Taddy Porter and Imperial Stout, are of exceptional quality. The two bottled organic beers have won the Soil Association's top awards three years in succession in 1999, 2000 and 2001. With the exception of Old Brewery Bitter, all Sam Smith's beers are now fined [clarified] with seaweed rather than isinglass. The seaweed is added during the copper boil with hops, and positive and negative charges in seaweed, hops and protein clear the beers. The beers are therefore suitable for vegans and vegetarians. Organic Best Ale has a superb recreation of a Victorian bottle label. In common with all Sam Smith's lagers, the organic version uses a Bavarian yeast strain.

Organic Lager (5% ABV)

Ingredients: pale lager malt, Vienna malt. German Hallertauer hop varieties.
Tasting note: gold/amber beer with a juicy malt and sweetcorn aroma, sweet malt and gentle hops in the mouth, and a finish that starts bitter-sweet but becomes dry and hoppy. Vienna malt, rarely used these days, even

in Austria, is a malt cured to a higher temperature than pale, and gives a dash of colour to lager beers and a rounded flavour.
Availability: bottled.

Organic Best Ale (5% ABV)

Ingredients: pale malt. New Zealand Hallertauer hops.
Tasting note: a true pale ale, using no darker malts, golden coloured, leading to an aroma dominated by tart citrus fruit similar to bitter blood oranges. Tart hops, citrus fruit and biscuity malt coat the tongue while the finish is intensely bitter, hoppy with sharp fruit.
Availability: bottled.

WYCHWOOD

Wychwood Brewery Co Ltd, Eagle Maltings, The Crofts, Corn Street, Witney, Oxon OX8 7AZ. Tel 01993 702574. Fax 01993 772553.
Email **intray@wychwood.co.uk** Website **www.wychwood.co.uk**

Wychwood is one Britain's most successful and enterprising small breweries. It has boosted production to 30,000 barrels a year – a phenomenal amount compared to most micro-brewers' output – and runs 31 pubs, many themed as Hobgoblinns after its flagship beer Hobgoblin. The company started as Glenny Brewery in 1983, based in the old maltings of the long-closed Clinch Brewery in Witney. Production moved to a new site in the late 1980s, and then back to Clinch's in 1994. The brewery now has a 110-barrel brew length.

Seventy per cent of production is bottled, using striking label images of goblins and other fantastic creatures. The Plumage Archer variety of barley malt used in Circle Master has long disappeared from the farming scene in

Britain, but a specialist maltster in Cambridge keeps seeds from all the varieties it has grown over the years. The seeds were propagated on a farm in Gloucestershire, and advice was given by experts in organic farming who work on the Prince of Wales's neighbouring Highgrove estate. English Organic Ale is the only canned beer in this guide: Sainsbury's says the packaging is appealing to younger customers.

English Organic Ale (4.5% ABV)

Brewed exclusively for Sainsbury's supermarkets.

Ingredients: Optic pale malt and wheat malt. German Hersbrucker, New Zealand Pacific Gem and English Target hops.

Tasting note: pale bronze beer with a rich biscuity malt aroma with some spicy hops, followed by creamy malt and tart hops on the tongue, and a big creamy malt and bitter hops finish.

Availability: canned.

Circle Master (4.7% ABV)

Ingredients: Plumage Archer pale malt. Target hops.

Tasting note: biscuity malt and citrus fruit dominate the aroma, with spicy hops in the mouth, and a long, lingering finish with sweet malt, a lemon drop citrus note, and spicy, bitter hops.

Availability: bottled.

Kiwi Organic Ale (5% ABV)

Brewed exclusively for Sainsbury's supermarkets.

Ingredients: Optic malt, crystal malt and wheat malt. New Zealand

Hallertauer and Pacific Gem hops.

Tasting note: Rich biscuity malt, spicy hops and a hint of cinnamon on the nose, juicy malt and tart hops in the mouth, and a long, intensely bitter finish with a good balance of malt and citrus fruit.

Availability: bottled.

The Organic Brewers of Germany

GERMANY

- •Hamburg
- Bremen •
- •Hannover ❷
- ❺
- Berlin
- •Dusseldorf
- •Leipzig
- Koln •
- Frankfurt •
- •Nurnberg ❹
- Saarbrucken •
- ❻
- • Stuttgart ❶❸
- ❼
- • Munich
- •Freiburg

KEY

1 Bucher (p.81)
2 Herrenhäuser (p.82)
3 Kronen (p.84)
4 Neumarkter Lammsbräu (p.85)
5 Pinkus Müller (p.87)
6 Riedenburger (p.89)
7 Adlerbrauerei (p.90)

Chapter 4

Organic Beers of Germany

German brewers keen to make the switch to organic production have a head start over their colleagues in other countries. German beers are covered by the *Reinheitsgebot* or Purity Law. If your beers are pure, then surely it is only a short and logical step to using organic materials to underscore that purity.

The law dates from 1516 and was introduced by the Bavarian royal family, the House of Wittelsbach, that ruled the independent south until it was deposed at the end of World War One. In 1516, dukes Wilhelm IV and Ludwig X introduced the purity law at an assembly of the Estates of the Realm at Ingolstadt. It laid down that only malted barley, yeast and water could be used to make beer. Hops were added to the law at a later stage when they began to be used widely in brewing.

The introduction of the *Reinheitsgebot* was not entirely altruistic. The Bavarian royal family, in the best feudal tradition, controlled barley production. It didn't want the monopoly weakened by the use of other cereals or sugars in the brewing process. In a country famous for its wheat beers, it is noticeable that that cereal was excluded from the original law. The reason was that the Bavarian aristocracy drank pale wheat beer at court, just as they consumed delicate white bread.

Brown beer made from barley was good enough for the masses, who also had to make do with inferior black bread. The mystique surrounding wheat beer was broken only in 1850 when the Wittelsbachs, whose power was in decline, licensed a Munich brewer to make the style for commercial sale in the Royal Court Brewery, the Hofbräuhaus. The Hofbräuhaus remains a major tourist attraction today, but is now owned by the state.

The *Reinheitsgebot* is still in force. It covers the whole of Germany including, again, the former East Germany. During the era of Communist rule, which ended soon after the fall of the Berlin Wall in 1989, East Germany abandoned the purity law.

In 1988, Michel Dubus, chairman of the French brewing group Fischer, successfully got the European Court to declare the *Reinheitsgebot* a "restraint of trade". As most of the large French brewers are based in the Strasbourg area just over the border, Debus and his colleagues were anxious to sell their beers in Germany. Until the court's declaration, they had been prevented from doing so as they use between 20 and 30 per cent of cereal adjuncts in their beers.

Far from being demolished, German brewers rallied to the cause of their purity law. Plaques appeared outside every brewery in the country – and there are some 1,200 of them – proclaiming that the beers were produced strictly to the terms of the purity law.

Newspaper articles railed against what they called "chemi-beers" from other countries. As a result, imported beers have made little headway in Germany, and the Czech Budweiser Budvar, which is brewed to the *Reinheitsgebot*, enjoys rather more consumer support there than American Budweiser.

Pinkus Müller (see Heroes of Organics), in common with Caledonian in Britain, was for years the lone standard bearer for organic beer in Germany. The numbers are growing slowly. It's likely, with such a large number of producers, that some small brewers have organic beers in their lockers for local consumption, but we list here those beers that enjoy wider distribution. In Germany, the organic certification authority is called Bioland.

Peter Hall (Hop Grower), of Marden, Kent: The only regular grower of organic hops in England, he says his organic Target variety taste better than hops grown with agri-chemicals.

Brakspear's: The elegant entrance to Brakspear's brewery in Henley-on-Thames. They brew four organic beers, one of which – Ted & Ben's – is named after to members of staff.

St Peter's: A modern plant is situated behind a medieval hall at this Suffolk brewery.

Shepherd Neame: The Faversham brewery, Britain's oldest, is based in the Kentish hop fields.

The malt store at Brakspear's: The brewing process unlocks vital sugars in malted barley.

"Taking a dip": A brewer at Greene King in Suffolk checks that brewing is progressing well.

St Peter's Brewery: Packaged beers come in unusual flagons based on an American design.

Pitfield: Martin Kemp runs the Pitfield Beer Shop and Brewery where all his beers are organic.

Duke of Cambridge, Islington: This was the world's first all-organic pub. The singhboulton company now has two more such pubs, one in East London and the other in West London.

Geetie Singh (left) & Esther Boulton: The founders of the London's organic pub chain.

Duke of Cambridge: The furniture and fittings in the main bar are all re-cycled.

Planet Organic: The West London shop has Britain's biggest selection of organic beers and ciders.

Cider apples: Ready to be picked and crushed, organic varieties are free from harmful sprays.

Thatchers: Modern technology ...   ... alongside traditional wooden vats.

BUCHER

Bucher GmbH, D-89423 Grundelfingen/Donau.
Tel 0049 9 073 95.98.0.
Email **abucher@bndlg.de** Website **www.brauerei-bucher.de**

There has been a brewery on the site since 1644. The present company, run by the Bucher family, dates from 1868, and the quality of the beer stems from the natural spring waters from the Grundelfinger Aloisius-Quelle in the Donau region. A new brewhouse, with stainless steel vessels, was installed in the 1970s. Bucher produces conventional lagers and wheat beers as well as its organic products. *Öko*, with *Bio*, are the German ways of expressing organic.

Öko-Bier (5.2% ABV)

Ingredients: pale Pilsner malt. Organic hops from the Hallertau.
Tasting note: a pale gold beer with a big citrus fruit and sweet malt aroma. There is tart lemon fruit in the mouth, with a big malty/fruity finish.
Availability: draught and bottled.

Organic Pilsner (5.2% ABV)

Ingredients: pale Pilsner malt. Organic hops from the Hallertau.
Tasting note: golden beer with a toasty and biscuity malt aroma, juicy malt and floral hops in the mouth, and a long bitter-sweet finish dominated by rich malt and tart hops.
Availability: draught and bottled.

HERRENHÄUSER

Brauerei Herrenhäuser, Herrenhäusen-strasse 83–99,
D-30419 Hannover. Tel 0049 511.7907.0.
Email **info@herrenhaeuser.de**   Website **www.herrenhaeuser.de**

Herrenhäuser is a major brewer in Hannover and its Pils is the biggest-selling version of the style in the region. The company was founded by the Middendorff family in 1868, and they are still in charge. Their Organic Lager is brewed to the style known as Märzen or March beer. Traditionally, this beer was brewed in Munich in March: before the industrial revolution and the development of ice-making machines, the early spring was the last time a beer could be brewed before warm temperatures and wild yeasts made fermentation impossible to control. March beers would then be stored until the autumn, when the casks were ceremonially tapped by the Mayor of Munich on the opening day of the world's most famous beer festival, the Oktoberfest.

Märzen beers were inspired by the work in the 19th century of the pioneering Austrian brewer Anton Dreher. Accompanied by the Munich brewer Gabriel Sedlmayr of the Spaten Brewery, Dreher as a young man toured all the great brewing capitals of Europe. The two men were impressed with the pale ales brewed in Britain, in Burton-on-Trent in particular. They went so far as to steal samples of yeast and fermenting beer by surreptitiously dipping hollow walking sticks into fermenting vessels. Dreher and Sedlmayr returned home, determined to use the new technologies of the Victorian age to fashion paler beers. Sedlmayr at Spaten was the first to introduce the lagering or cold-storage of beer on a commercial scale, but he was frustrated by the devotion of local people to dark or Dunkel beer.

While Pilsen in Bohemia was the first brewing city to produce a truly pale, golden beer by the cold-fermentation process, Dreher developed a style known as Vienna Red or Amber. The basis of his beer was a malt cured at a slightly higher temperature than either English pale malt or Pilsner malt used in Bohemia. The finished beer had an attractive translucent amber-red colour. Its success was considerable, and Dreher opened breweries in Hungary and Italy to make his beers available to a wider audience. In Munich, Gabriel Sedlmayr's brother Josef, who owned the Franziskaner Brewery, produced his own version of Vienna Red, and this became the touchstone for the March beers developed by all the brewers in the city for the Oktoberfest.

Vienna Red was short-lived. It is brewed today by only a couple of Austrian breweries. In Munich, Märzen has largely disappeared, and has been replaced by lagers called Oktoberfest. They are brewed for the beer festival, but are stored for a shorter period, and are pale in colour, offered in the main to visitors from other countries with little knowledge of true Oktoberfest beers.

Brewers in other parts of Germany produce a few traditional March beers, and it is good to see Herrenhäuser making one, though it is a shade too pale to be true to style.

Premium Organic Lager (5.3% ABV)

Ingredients: pale Pilsner malt and Munich malt. Organic hops from the Hallertau.

Tasting note: burnished gold colour, with a rich and enticing fresh corn, citrus fruit and tart hops aroma. Juicy, biscuity malt and delicate hop bitterness dominate the palate, while the finish has a delightful lemon-jelly fruitiness balancing malt and hops. A superb beer.

Availability: draught and bottled.

KRONEN

Kronenbrauerei Rudolf Wahl KG, Professor-Bamann-strasse 20, D-89423, Gundelfingen/Donau. Tel 0049.9073.73.58.
Email **info@kronenbrauerei.de**
Websites **www.kronenbrauerei.de** and **www.cannabia.de**

There are several German breweries with Kronen in the name – it means "crown". This Kronen brewery, a neighbour of Bucher's in the Gundelfingen area, was founded in 1543 and is still in the hands of the Wahl family. The present brewmaster, Rudolf Wahl, is a lively, enthusiastic 68-year-old who has converted some of his beers to organic production in recent years.

He achieved a degree of notoriety when he agreed to brew a beer with hemp in 1996. This followed a decision by the government to authorise the cultivation of hemp. It is a member of the same plant family as cannabis – as is the hop (too many hops in beer can have a soporific effect). Herr Wahl points out that hemp was widely used in beer until the *Reinheitsgebot* was introduced in 1516. He uses more hemp flowers than hops in his Cannabia. The character of all the Kronen beers is determined by the fine spring waters that flow down from the Bavarian mountains.

Ökokrone Export (5% ABV)
Ingredients: pale Pilsner malt. Organic hops from the Hallertau.
Tasting note: pale gold beer with a tempting biscuity malt

and spicy hops aroma, with crisp hops in the mouth, followed by a long and quenching malty/hoppy finish.
Availability: draught and bottled.

Cannabia (5% ABV)

Ingredients: pale Pilsner malt. Organically-grown hemp flowers and organic hops from the Hallertau.
Tasting note: golden beer with a grassy, floral and herbal aroma, with a full-bodied malt and hemp palate, and a long spicy finish balanced by juicy malt.
Availability: draught and bottled.

NEUMARKTER LAMMSBRÄU

Brauerei Neumarkter Lammsbräu, Gebr. Ehrnsperger e.K, Amberger-strasse 1, D-92318 Neumarkt. Tel 0049 918 404.0.
Email **info@lammsbraeu.de** Website **www.lammsbraeu.de**

The brewery started life as an inn called the Golden Lamb in 1628 in Neumarkt (Newmarket), a town famous for pencil production some 40km (25 miles) south of Nuremberg. When Franz Ehrnsperger took over the family brewery he was determined to use only organically-grown materials. He was told by other brewers that it was impossible to brew beers purer than those that adhere to the *Reinheitsgebot*.

But he believes passionately in living in harmony with nature. He says that malt and hops grown without fertilisers and pesticides have a cleaner, fresher taste, while organic hops develop a finer aroma.

Herr Ehrnsperger has encouraged a group of farmers to produce organic barley and wheat to his specification. Hop growers have also set aside areas for organic hop cultivation. Land had to lie fallow for three years before organic cereals and hops could be grown, and it took a further five years for the required quality to develop. Herr Erhnsperger is a patron of the arts, supporting local opera.

Helles Hefeweizen (5.1% ABV)

Ingredients: pale malted barley and malted wheat. Organic hops from the Hallertau.

Tasting note: hazy gold colour, with a creamy malt and pronounced hint of banana on the aroma, tart fruit, creamy malt and spicy hops on the tongue, and a rich malty finish balanced by banana fruit, with a hoppiness that finally becomes dry.

Availability: draught and bottled.

NB *Helles* means "pale" while *hefeweizen* indicates a white or wheat beer matured with yeast (*hefe*) in the bottle.

Kristall Weizen (5.1% ABV)

Ingredients: pale malted barley and malted wheat. Organic hops from the Hallertau.

Tasting note: golden beer with a hint of bronze, a rich malt and banana fruit aroma, with mellow malt, creamy fruit and spicy hops in the mouth, followed by a crisp, quenching finish dominated by rich malt, tart fruit and tangy hops.

Availability: draught and bottled.

NB Kristall indicates that the beer is filtered to remove the yeast.

Edel Pils (5.2% ABV)

Ingredients: pale Pilsner malt. Organic hops from the Hallertau.

Tasting note: pale gold beer with a juicy, biscuity malt aroma balanced by spicy hops and a hint of lemon fruit. The palate is a fine balance between juicy malt and tart hops, while the lingering finish starts malty, with a touch of tart fruit, but is finally dominated by gently bitter hops.

Availability: draught and bottled.

NB *Edel* means "noble"; it reflects the domination of brewing by the nobility in the medieval period; in modern times, hop growers in the mighty Hallertau call their plants "noble hops" as they believe they have the finest aroma and flavour.

PINKUS MÜLLER

Brauerei Pinkus Müller, 4–10 Kreuz-strasse, D-48143 Münster, Nordrhein-Westfalen. Tel 0049 251 45151, 0049 251 45152. Fax: 0049 251 57136

Email **info@pinkus-mueller.de**   Website **www.pinkus-mueller.de**

(See Heroes of Organics). This world-famous brew-tavern, bakery and chocolate-maker in the ancient university city of Münster is the flag-bearer for organic beer in Germany, and its beers are widely exported to other European countries and to the United States. The beers can be enjoyed in the charming, rustic restaurant attached to the brewery, where dishes are cooked with the beers.

Original (5% ABV)

Ingredients: pale malted barley and wheat malt. Organic hops from the Hallertau.

Tasting note: golden beer with a rich creamy, buttery malt aroma balanced by crisp hops. Rich malt and spicy hops dominate the finish, followed by refreshing creamy malt and tart hops in the finish.

Availability: draught and bottled.

NB The label describes this beer as *obergärig*, which means top-fermenting. The beer is an *Alt* or old beer, the type brewed before lagering and cold-fermentation in the 19th century. Düsseldorf is the city most closely associated with Alt, but the Pinkus version is different due to the use of 40 per cent malted wheat; it reflects the style of beer brewed in Münster before the rise of lager.

Pinkus Spezial (5.1% ABV)

Ingredients: pale malted barley. Organic hops from the Hallertau.

Tasting note: burnished gold colour, with a malty/toffee aroma balanced by floral hops. There are tangy hops in the mouth with citrus fruit, followed by a long quenching finish dominated by spicy hops with a gentle hint of citrus.

Availability: draught and bottled.

Hefe Weizen (5.2% ABV)

Ingredients: pale barley malt and malted wheat. Organic hops from the Hallertau.

Tasting note: hazy gold colour, with a dense, rocky head, a floral hops and creamy malt aroma, a quenching, tart palate with hints of rich fruit, and a big finish balanced between malt, floral hops and creamy fruit.

Availability: draught and bottled.

RIEDENBURGER

Riedenburger Bräuhaus, Michael Krieger KG, Hammerweg 5, D-93339 Riedenburg. Tel 0049 9442 644.
Email **riedenburger@gmx.de** Website **www.riedenburger.de**

Michael Krieger's small family-owned brewery is in the beautiful Bavarian Altmühltal, the waterway that links the Rhine and the Danube rivers. The brewery is just a few kilometres north of the world's greatest hop-growing area, the Hallertau.

Organic Lager (4.6% ABV)
Ingredients: pale Pilsner malt. Organic hops from the Hallertau.
Tasting note: golden beer with a biscuity malt and floral hops aroma, quenching malt in the mouth balanced by spicy hops, and a long finish that begins with a sweet malt note but becomes dry and hoppy.
Availability: draught and bottled.

ADLERBRAUEREI

Adlerbrauerei Göggingen, Vertriebs GmbH, Kirchweg 2, OT: Göggingen, D–72505 Krauchenwies. Tel: 0049 7576 978.
Fax 0049 7576 97888. Website **www.biobier.com**

Adlerbrauerei brews three organic beers under the name of Binger Lamm

Bräu. They were not available for tasting and are not exported. They are:

Bioland Pilsner (4.9% ABV)

Bioland Woiza (5.2% ABV: a wheat beer)

Bioland Schwarzes Schäfle (5.4% ABV: a dark beer).

Chapter 5

Organic Beers of France

France has two disparate brewing traditions. The
Strasbourg area of Alsace has long been disputed
territory: the people are of French and German
descent. The city was independent until seized by
France in 1681, it was then part of Germany from
1871 to 1919, and again during the Nazi occupation
in World War Two.

Not surprisingly, brewing there has been heavily influenced by German
practice, and production is geared to lager beer, with such familiar brand
names as Kronenbourg, Fischer and Pelforth. Kronenbourg, far and away the
biggest beer brand in France, is now owned by Britain's major brewer,
Scottish Courage, while Pelforth is owned by Heineken. The beers of Alsace
come from modern plants with stainless steel vessels, computer controls,
and fast production methods: the term *lager*, which means "to store" in
German, is only a nominal term where French versions of the style are
concerned.

The other tradition, in the Nord-Pas de Calais region that stretches from
the English Channel ports to Lille, could not be more different. The people
of the region have powerful Flemish roots. They prefer the name "French
Flanders", and they have a somewhat ambivalent attitude to the rest of the

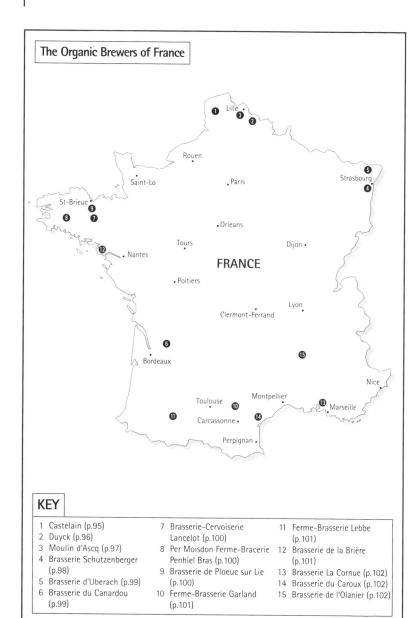

The Organic Brewers of France

FRANCE

Lille
Rouen
Saint-Lo
Paris
Strasbourg
St-Brieuc
Orleans
Tours
Dijon
Nantes
Poitiers
Lyon
Clermont-Ferrand
Bordeaux
Nice
Toulouse
Montpellier
Marseille
Carcassonne
Perpignan

republic. Lille was once the capital of Flanders, and every summer the people of Douai take to the streets to celebrate a medieval victory over ... the French.

The brewers of French Flanders are small producers. They call themselves "artisanal brewers". Many of them originated on farms, where beer-making was part of the natural, seasonal way of life, and helped refresh farmers, their families and their labourers. Their beer styles pre-date the industrial revolution, with March, autumn and winter beers. They come under the general name of *bières de garde*. It means "keeping beers" or "stored beers", but they are warm-fermenting members of the ale family, not German-style lagers.

Historically, *bières de garde* were made in March, the last time brewing could take place before warm weather meant uncontrollable fermentation temperatures and spoilage by wild yeasts. The beers were strong, protected by alcohol and hops, and made from cereals and hops in the surrounding fields. They were drunk during the summer and, in particular, during the heavy work of harvest time. Then, when new grain and hops had been harvested in the autumn, the brewing cycle would start again.

For most of the 20th century, the beers of French Flanders quietly stagnated. At the start of that century, there were 3,000 breweries throughout France. By 1976, the number had fallen to 76, and then to 33 by the 1990s. The decline was the result of the twin assault by wine and lager beer. Lager in particular came under the control of brewing giants with the ability to mass market their products, and mask the different tradition of brewing in the Flanders region. Then the brewing worm turned. In the 1980s students in Lille started to proclaim the pleasures of a *bière de garde* called Jenlain, from a hamlet of the same name near Valenciennes.

The Duyck family that owned the brewery had started to bottle Jenlain in attractive corked and wire-cradled bottles, whereas most small brewers in the region – rather like English farm cider makers – merely offered draught beers sold at the farm gate. Jenlain launched a cult. People discovered a handful of other brewers still patiently producing *bières de garde*. Others were encouraged to remove the sacks and tarpaulins from unused equipment, and fire their coppers again. Inspired by the revival, others launched brand-new breweries, or attached them to existing bars and restaurants. An organisation called *Les Amis de la Bière* – the Friends of Beer – produced books and pamphlets on the traditions of French Flanders, and staged regular beer festivals. Enthusiasm spread, and today there are new small breweries in Brittany and even the grape-growing south.

Surprisingly, given its reputation for fine food and drink, France has been slow to adopt organic production. In 1997, the government, alarmed by fast food (*la mal-bouffe*), launched a campaign to encourage the French – the young in particular – to pay more attention to what they consume. There has been a knock-on effect, with a small but growing demand for organic produce. It is hard work for brewers. At the moment, there is not a single maltster in the whole of France able to supply organic grain, and brewers have to go instead to Belgium and Germany for their supplies. A few farmers are growing organic hops, but the majority of hops used in organic beers come from Austria and Germany. Beers that meet EU rules for organic labelling are authorised by the French equivalent of the Soil Association known as Ecocert.

Listed below are three brewers in Nord-Pas de Calais whose organic beers are available in Britain, France and other European countries. They are followed by a list, compiled by Aymeric Gillet and Gwenaël Samotyj of ATPUB (*Association Pour l'Union des Bièrophiles*: Society for the Unity of Beerlovers), of breweries producing organic beer for local domestic consumption. Some make use of the EU rule that permits a maximum of five per cent non-organic ingredients, which usually means hops.

CASTELAIN

Brasserie Castelain, 13 rue Pasteur, Bénifontaine, 62410 Wingles.
Tel 0030.3.21.08.68.68.

Email **contact@chti.com** Website **www.chit.com**

Tours by appointment Tuesday to Friday and without appointment Saturday morning 9.00–11.00. There is a small charge, which includes a beer.

Yves Castelain, the first brewer of organic beer in France, has been at the forefront of the revival of traditional brewing. The village of Bénifontaine, north of Lens, was once at the heart of the northern coal fields that featured in Emile Zola's tragic novel *Germinal*. The brewery, with its burnished coppers visible from the road outside – aptly named rue Pasteur – was a farm brewery dating from 1926. It supplied miners as well as land workers. It once had a beer called Prolétarienne, with a cheeful mine worker on the label holding a foaming glass. The label on the main range of beers, called Ch'ti, also once featured a miner, but he went from black to grey, and finally faded away as the last pits closed. Ch'ti is the local Picardy way of saying "*c'est toi*" – it suits you.

As well as the Ch'ti beers and Jade, Castelain honours the patron saint of brewers, Saint Arnold, with a Sint Arnoldus monastic-style beer. A wooden carving of the saint hangs in the brewhouse. The brewery produces around 50,000 hectolitres a year, and is a wonderfully convivial place.

The workforce gathers in the brewhouse on Fridays for a beery get-together, and retired members of the Castelain family drop in for a party every autumn when the Christmas beers are launched. Yves Castelain's watchwords are: "*Nous préservons toujours l'authentique"* – in other words, "We preserve authenticity."

Jade (4.5% ABV)

Ingredients: Belgian pale and amber malts. Aurora and Perler hops.

Tasting note: burnished gold colour, with a big spicy hop and tart fruit aroma, rich juicy malt in the mouth balanced by spicy hops and citrus fruit, with a long finish balanced beautifully between biscuity malt, bitter hops and orange fruit. The beer is authorised by Ecocert.

Availability: bottled.

DUYCK

Brasserie Duyck, 113 rue Nationale, 59144 Jenlain.

Tel 0030.3.27.49/70.03.

Email **contact@duyck.com** Website **www.duyck.com**

The brewery is not open to visitors, but the beers can be enjoyed at its specialist bar and restaurant Café Jenlain, 43 place Rihour, 59800 Lille.

The name Duyck declares the Flemish origins of the family, though the brewery is better known to an international audience by the name of its main beer, Jenlain. The brewery, typical of the region, started life to refresh the farmer and his workers. Félix Duyck, son of a farmer-brewer from Zeggers-Cappel in Flanders, took over the brewery in 1922. Eventually brewing replaced farming, and today Félix's son Robert and grandson Raymond are in charge.

Duyck is responsible for the world-wide interest in *bière de garde*. The company broke the draught mould in the late 1960s by putting Jenlain into attractive Champagne-style stoppered and wired-cradled bottles. The result is impressive: production has grown from 15,000 hectolitres a year in the 1970s to 90,000 today. Jenlain has been followed by spring and Christmas brews.

In 1994 Duyck introduced a new beer called Sebourg, named after a neighbouring village, where wheat used to be milled: wheat as well as barley malt is used in the beer. This was followed by St Druon de Sebourg, named after a monk (1118–1186) who founded a monastery there. The latest beer, introduced in 1998, is Fraîche de l'Aunelle, an organic beer named after a stream that runs through Jenlain and Sebourg, and which powered the mill.

Fraîche de l'Aunelle (5.5% ABV)

Ingredients: Belgian and German pale malts, unmalted wheat. Hallertauer Perler and Tradition hop varieties.

Tasting note: hazy blond colour. Pronounced fruit aroma with a spicy hop note. Chewy malt, peppery hops, fruit and spices in the mouth, with a big finish in which bready malt, chewy grain, tart fruit and spicy hops vie for attention. The beer is authorised by Ecocert.

Availability: bottled.

MOULIN D'ASCQ

Brasserie Artisanale du Moulin d'Ascq, route de Sainghin, 59650 Villeneuve d'Ascq. Tel 0030.3.20.41.58.48.
Email **moulindascq@aol.com**

In spite of the rustic name, this is a new small brewery that opened in the suburbs of Lille in the late 1990s. It launched its first organic beer, Blonde, in 1999, and followed it with an amber version in 2001.

Blonde (6.2% ABV)

Ingredients: pale Pilsner malt. Hallertauer and Perler hop varieties from Bavaria.

Tasting note: golden colour with a pronounced biscuity malt and citrus fruit aroma. Juicy malt, spicy hops and tart fruit dominate the palate, while the lingering finish becomes dry and bitter after a malty and fruity start.

Availability: bottled.

Ambrée (6.6% ABV)

Ingredients: pale Pilsner malt and Munich malt. Hallertauer and Perler hop varieties from Bavaria.

Tasting note: burnished copper colour, with a big nutty and fruity aroma balanced by rich grain. A firm-bodied palate offers dark sultana fruit, spicy hops, hints of chocolate and ripe malt, while the finish has chewy grain, dark and bitter fruit, and peppery hops.

Availability: bottled. The beers, authorised by Ecocert, are refermented in the bottle with the addition of malt syrup.

Domestic Producers

Some domestic brewers are extremely small, as the word *ferme* (farm) in the names indicates.

ALSACE

Brasserie Schutzenberger

8 rue de la Patrie, 67300 Schiltigheim. Tel 0030 3.88.18.61.00.

La Bio (5% ABV ABV)

The beer is neither filtered nor pasteurised. Authorised by Ecocert.

Brasserie d'Uberach

30 Grande Rue, 67350 Uberach. Tel 0030.3.88.07.07.77.

Mielusine (4.8% ABV)

Haute Yutz (4.8% ABV)

The beers are neither filtered nor pasteurised. Authorised by Ecocert.

AQUITAINE

Brasserie du Canardou

La Pendue, 24610 Villefranche de Lonchat. Tel 0030.5.53.80.55.54.
Email **canardou@wanadoo.fr**

The beers are made by British-style infusion mashing and the russet-coloured La Korlène is inspired by English ale.

La Dame Blanche (4% ABV)

La Félibrée (5% ABV)

Al'Aven (5% ABV)

La Korlène (6% ABV)

La Nonnette (6% ABV)

The beers are neither filtered nor pasteurised. Authorised by Ecocert.

BRITTANY

Brasserie-Cervoiserie Lancelot

Site de la Mine d'Or, 56460 Le Roc St-André.
Tel 0030 2.97.74.74.74.
Email **brasserie.lancelot@libertysurf.fr**
Website **www.cervoiserie-lancelot.com**

Pays de Cocagne (5.5% ABV)

Natural Mystic (5.8% ABV)

Authorised by Ecocert.

Per Moisdon Ferme-Bracerie Penhiel Bras

56630 Langonnet. Tel 0030.2.97.23.64.84.
Email **per.moisdon@wanadoo.fr**

Bière du Chardon (6.5% ABV)

Authorised by Ecocert.

Brasserie de Ploeuc sur Lie

Les Norniers, 22150 Ploeuc sur Lie. Tel 0030.2.96.64.27.47.

La Oezett (5% ABV)

MIDI-PYRENEES

Ferme-Brasserie Garland

Christian Garland, Les Pesquies, 81470 Algans.
Tel 0030.5.63.75.74.68.

Karland Ambrée (6% ABV)

Kan Bière (6% ABV)

Ferme-Brasserie Lebbe

Pierre Lebbe, Lieu dit Le Village, 65700 Villefranque.
Tel 0030.5.62.96.47.27.

L'Amalthée (6% ABV)

PAYS DE LOIRE

Brasserie de la Brière

Le Nézyl, 44410 St-Lyphard. Tel 0030 2.40.91.33.62.
Email **brasserie.briere:wanadoo.fr**
Website **www.brasserie-de-la-briere.fr**

Thorella (5.5% ABV)
Authorised by Ecocert.

PROVENCE-ALPES-CÔTE D'AZUR

Brasserie La Cornue

Jean Jacques Cornue & Fils, Chemin de Valadet, 13032 Eguilles.
Tel 0030.4.42.29.75.01.

These beers are conditioned in bottle. The hops are not certified organic.

Ginger Ale (5.5% ABV)

Blanche (6.1% ABV)

Tex Mex (6.5% ABV)

Blonde (6.9% ABV)

Ambrée (7.5% ABV)

Brune (7.9% ABV)

LANGUEDOC-ROUSSILLON

Brasserie du Caroux

10 avenue Albert Marcelin, 34800 Nebian. Tel 0030.4.67.88.40.07.

La Blanche Legère (5.9% ABV)

La Cervoise **(6.9% ABV)**

La Carousse **(6.9% ABV)**

La Blanche **(6.9% ABV)**
Authorised by Ecocert.

RHÔNE-ALPES

Brasserie de l'Olanier
L'Olanier Beaumont, 07260 Joyeuse. Tel 0030.4.75.39.56.90.

La Joyeuse Blonde **(7.5% ABV)**

La Joyeuse Ambrée **(7.5% ABV)**

La Joyeuse Brune **(7.5% ABV)**
Authorised by Ecocert.

Chapter 6
Organic Beers of Belgium

Belgium is arguably the most fascinating of the world's great brewing nations. Historically, culturally and linguistically divided, Flemish and French speakers are united by their passion for beer. The choice available to them is remarkable. Belgians may quaff large amounts of everyday lager beers, such as Stella Artois and Jupiler, but it's the speciality sector that is growing. The country is famous for the beers produced by six monastic breweries attached to Trappist abbeys.

The success of the monks' ales has prompted a flood of copy-cat "Abbey beers" from commercial breweries. There has been a revival of interest in *saison* – or seasonal ales – that originated on farms, and which have clear similarities to the *bières de garde* in French Flanders.

Wheat or white beers, often brewed with the addition of fruit and spices, have found favour in both Belgium and Britain. The Hoegaarden brand in

The Organic Brewers of Belgium

Bruges •

• Antwerp

•Ghent

• Kortrijk

• Brussels

BELGIUM

• Liege

❶

• Mons

• Namur

KEY

1 Dupont (p.106)

particular has become something of a cult drink among young people in both countries. Fruit, in the form of cherries and raspberries, is added to the amazing lambic and gueuze beers brewed in the Payottenland area centred on Brussels. The beers are made by "spontaneous fermentation", with wild yeasts allowed to impregnate the sugar-rich extract known as wort. The beers are stored in oak tuns for a year or several years, and fruit is added to some of the batches.

The Belgians are great admirers of British beer, and they have fashioned some magnificent pale ales along British lines, though the Belgian versions tend to be both stronger and hoppier. De Koninck from Antwerp is unquestionably the classic of Belgian pale ales. There are brown beers, too, of which Liefmans is the best-known producer. In West Flanders, "sour red" beers, which may have a link to the early porter beers of England, are stored in unlined oak vessels where they are infected by wild yeasts and other organisms.

Organic beer has made little headway in Belgium. This may be due to the undoubted quality of the existing products and the pride Belgians feel towards them. Organic barley and hops are being grown in the country, and it is hoped that, encouraged by the growth of chemical-free beers in neighbouring countries, Belgium will follow the trend.

DUPONT

Brasserie Dupont, 5 Rue Basse, B-7904 Tourpes-Leuze.
Tel 0032 69.67.10.66.
Email **contact@brasserie-dupont.com**
Website **www.brasserie-dupont.com**

The Dupont brewery, a short journey from the city of Tournai on the Franco-Belgian border, is on a farm in flat, bleak countryside where the occasional tree stands like a lonely sentinel. The farm is blessed with a natural spring that provides excellent brewing water. Dupont is acclaimed as the classic producer of *saison*, the Belgian rustic style that originated on farms and sustained those working in the fields during the summer and the harvest.

Founded in 1850, the brewery has been run by the Dupont family since the 1920s. Marc Roisier, a grandson on the distaff side, is now in charge and produces around 6,500 hectolitres a year, a surprisingly modest amount for such a distinguished company. Close to a quarter of the annual production is exported to Britain, Canada, France, Italy, Japan and the United States.

The small, steam-filled and strictly artisan brewhouse uses pale and caramalts, with Kent Goldings and Styrian Goldings hop varieties for its main brands. In the tradition of *saison* breweries, the mash tun has a double role. First, the malt is mixed with hot water to make a mash. When malt starch has been converted into sugar, the sweet "wort" is run off from the tun into a collecting vessel, and the used grains are dug out, and the vessel cleaned. The wort is then pumped back into the tun where it is boiled with hops.

A 6.5% *saison* is called Vieille Provision: translated from the French, the name Old Provision underscores the heritage of a style that was important to the farmers' nutrition and diet. It has an intense peppery hoppiness, a hazy gold colour and dense collar of foam. The 9.2% Christmas seasonal is called Avec Les Bons Voeux de la Brasserie – a mouthful in every way. The name means, "With the best wishes of the brewery."

Dupont also brews beers under the Moinette label. They are named after Marc Rosier's farm, which is thought to stand on the site of a former monastery: *moinette* means "little monk". There are organic versions of both the saison and the Moinette beers, and also a beer in which organic honey (*miel*) is used both for flavour and to encourage a strong fermentation: one of the first beers brewed by the Duponts in the 1920s used honey. This is another ancient tradition: like the Founding Fathers in America, farmers used whatever cereals and ingredients were to hand to fashion their beers.

In addition to the beers, Dupont produces bread and cheese, and all the products are available for sale in a shop across the road from the main entrance to the brewery. A statue of Saint Arnold, the patron saint of brewers, watches over Dupont's activities from the farm yard.

Saison Dupont Bio (5.5%)

Ingredients: pale malt. Belgian and German hop varieties.

Tasting note: hazy-gold colour, with a big peppery/spicy aroma balanced by biscuity malt, a full malty palate with tart hops and some citrus fruit, and a long, intense finish balanced between juicy malt, bitter, spicy hops and tart fruit.

Availability: bottled.

Moinette Biologique Blonde (7.5%)

Ingredients: pale malt. Belgian and German hop varieties.

Tasting note: pale gold with a massive, booming aroma of spicy hops, ripe malt and tart fruit, a rich palate of juicy malt, tangy hops and orange fruit, and a long finish in which malt, hops and citrus fruit vie for attention.

Availability: bottled.

Moinette Biologique Ambrée (7.5%)

Ingredients: pale and caramalts. Belgian and German hop varieties.

Tasting note: russet beer with a nutty, fruity and chocolatey aroma balanced by tart hops, a rich, full-bodied malty palate with dark fruit and chocolate notes, and a long finish that starts bitter-sweet and creamy, but becomes dry, with bitter fruit and hops dominating.

Availability: bottled.

Bière de Miel Ambrée (8%)

Ingredients: pale and caramalts, with organic honey. Belgian and German hop varieties.

Tasting note: the beer is similar to the dark version of Moinette Biologique, but has a smooth, satiny honey sweetness on the aroma, palate and finish.
Availability: bottled.
NB The beers are authorised by Biogarantie.

Chapter 7

Organic Beers
of the United States

The United States has undergone a brewing revolution in the past 20 years, a revolution that has challenged the hegemony of international giants such as Anheuser-Busch, the brewer of Budweiser, and which has restored choice and diversity to drinkers. On the back of the beer renaissance, a handful of craft brewers are now fashioning beers made with organic materials.

The Founding Fathers from England brought with them an ale tradition. The "second wave" of immigrants from Central Europe augmented that tradition with the new techniques of lager brewing. Germans in particular built a dominant presence in the brewing industry. With the arrival of the railroad, they were able to sell beer on a much wider scale, and to a less discriminating audience. Lager beers became blander, adulterated with cheaper cereals such as corn and rice, and with a decreasing level of hops.

The domination of the new national brewers was intensified by

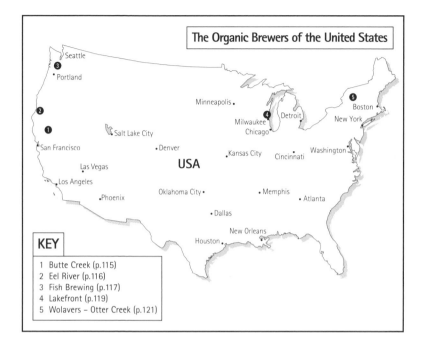

The Organic Brewers of the United States

Seattle
3
Portland

2
1
San Francisco
Las Vegas
Los Angeles
Phoenix

Salt Lake City

Minneapolis

Milwaukee **4** Detroit
Chicago

Denver
Kansas City Cincinnati
USA
Oklahoma City Memphis
Atlanta
Dallas
New Orleans
Houston

Boston **5**
New York
Washington

KEY

1 Butte Creek (p.115)
2 Eel River (p.116)
3 Fish Brewing (p.117)
4 Lakefront (p.119)
5 Wolavers – Otter Creek (p.121)

Prohibition. During the 13 years between 1920 and 1933, when the manufacture of alcohol was banned, only the biggest breweries survived by selling ice-cream, malted milk and yeast. Prohibition was replaced by the Great Depression, which closed still more breweries. And then a generation of young potential beer drinkers spent the Second World War abroad. The stranglehold of such national brewers as Anheuser-Busch, Coors, Miller and Schlitz seemed unbreakable.

But from the 1960s, and with gathering pace in the decades that followed, a counter-culture has developed. Small "micro-brewers", many of them home-brewers who went the extra mile to brew commercially, started to fashion ales and lagers based on original recipes. Some of the pioneers of the craft brewing movement were inspired by British beer, pale ale in particular. Then the micros had their own "second wave" as other craft brewers, fascinated by the great beers of the Czech Republic and Germany, offered an alternative to the likes of Budweiser with genuine cold-fermented lagers. Still more drew their inspiration from the scintillating ales, including monastic beers, made in Belgium.

Today there are some 1,300 breweries in the US, more than in Germany. In a country where just one brand, Budweiser, accounts for half the beer made there, the micros account for only one or two per cent of beer sales. But their impact outweighs their size, and even the giants have had to respond to consumer demand by making beer truer to style, and with some malt and hop character.

Craft brewers are concerned with quality. Many are keen environmentalists, who recycle used grains and hops, and treat water to remove chemicals that can affect the aroma and flavour of their beers. It's a short step to making organic beer. The only problems have been lack of raw materials, and insufficient sales to make production feasible. In the early 1990s a couple of brewers, one in Indiana, a second in New York City, launched organic lagers but with little success. An all-organic brewery, Humes Brewing Company, in Glen Allen, California, ran from 1993 to 2001, but founder Peter Humes found the work so labour intensive and the income so negligible that he was unable to continue.

The organic sector's presence was minimal and declining, but it was given an urgent transfusion by the impact of imports from Europe. Sales of Pinkus Müller's beers from Germany grew by nearly 50 per cent a year in the late 1990s and early 2000s. The Seattle-based Merchant Du Vin, which also owns the acclaimed Pike Place micro, has been importing Samuel Smith's ales from Yorkshire for several years, and has now added the English brewery's organic ale and lager. Caledonian Brewery's Golden Promise, the first and biggest-selling organic beer in Britain, has built a presence in the US, and has been joined by another Scottish beer, Broughton's Border Gold.

American brewers keen to follow the European trend were encouraged by the domestic growth in sales of organic food and drink. The organic food industry recorded sales of $6 billion in 1999, and that figure is expected to rise to $13 billion by 2003. It's small beer in a country the size of the United

States, but it's a sector that is growing, and can now offer the sustaining income that failed to materialise in the early 1990s.

In the land that has pioneered genetically modified cereals, fruit and vegetables, a tiny but vocal group of producers and consumers are turning away from the Frankenstein view of the future offered by the likes of Monsanto. Supporters of organics prefer to live in harmony with nature rather than perverting it. As in Britain, organic produce is no longer confined to farmers' markets or the backs of trucks. It's on supermarket shelves and is bought by city folk as well as country dwellers. With growing concerns about the hazards of mass-produced food, the epidemics that result from intensive farming, and the growth of vegetarianism and veganism, the demand for organic produce is no longer confined to the better off.

There's a price to pay, though. Organic malt costs around 30 per cent more than conventional grain. Supplies are now available from North America, which lowers transport costs. Some comes from the Canadian prairies of Saskatchewan, other from within the US itself. A specialist malting supplier, Bioriginal, deals only in pale malt. Briess Malting in Chilton, Wisconsin, offers a choice of speciality malts, including caramalt, Munich and chocolate, along with roasted barley: the last named is widely used in American interpretations of Irish stout. But the lack of specific items can be frustrating. Charlie Hawks of Hawks Brewing in Roseburg, Oregon, would like to make a Belgian-style Tripel, using organic materials, but he can't get supplies of Pilsner malt or candy sugar.

Hops are a bigger problem. The main hop-growing areas of the United States are Idaho's Snake River Valley, Oregon's Willamette Valley, and Washington State east of the Cascade mountains and principally in the Yakima Valley. Washington accounts for some 70 per cent of hop production. Unlike rain-soaked England, the Pacific North-west enjoys bountiful sunshine, but it also has its share of attack from spider mites, aphids and powdery mildew. Hop farmers respond with the spray can, killing ladybugs (the American name for the ladybird) and other predators that are the worst enemy of pests.

As in Britain, American brewers of organic beer have to turn to Germany, and New Zealand for supplies of Pacific Gem and Hallertauer. They are fine hops, but they are far removed from the likes of home-grown Cascade, Centennials, Chinook, Columbus and Willamette, which add distinctive piney, peppery, and citrus aromas and flavours to American beers. Some American hops are used, however: brewers in the United States are given the same opt-out as their European brethren and can use five per cent of "agricultural material" that is not organic. As hops usually make up less than that proportion of the ingredients in beer, conventional hops are used in some beers labelled organic.

There's one more mountain to climb: certification. At present there is no national body, such as Britain's Soil Association or Germany's Bioland, though the Department of Agriculture is studying possible regulations. Brewers for the time being have to register with local state bodies. The splendidly-named Oregon Tilth (tilth is an Old English word for tilling the soil) certifies organic food and drink in the state. In common with similar organisations, Oregon Tilth, a non profit-making body, needs written confirmation that all ingredients (with the five per cent opt-out) are organic. Cereals must come from land that has been chemical-free for at least three years. It then examines the brewery to ensure that all cleaning materials are approved, and organic and non-organic materials are segregated. Oregon Tilth requires its clients to pay $5,000 of the first $1 million of sales, and 0.1 per cent of sales after that. Some small brewers, such as Butte Creek in Chico, California, don't bother to seek certification as they say sales don't warrant the expense.

In spite of difficulties in obtaining materials, and the necessary but tedious business of certification, the new organic brewers are enjoying more success than the trail-blazers of the early 1990s. It's likely that many more craft brewers will join the ranks. As for the nationals, don't stand in line just yet for the first batch of Organic Bud. As well as finding sufficient quantities of malt and hops, Anheuser-Busch would also have to source supplies of organic rice. A-B are proud of the stuff: they list it first on their labels.

BUTTE CREEK

Butte Creek Brewery, 945 West Second Street, Chico, California 95928. Tel 530 894 7906.
Email **butte@buttecreek.com** Website **www.buttecreek.com**

Butte [as in "beaut"] Creek was founded in 1996, with production in the hands of experienced brewer Roland Allen, who has worked at his craft for 15 years, and included a spell at what he, tongue-in-cheek, calls "Chico's other brewery". This is a reference to Sierra Nevada, one of the biggest and most acclaimed craft breweries in the US. Roland's partners are Tom Atmore and Bill Beeghly. Butte Creek's brewhouse can knock out 3,000 barrels a year, but demand for its beers, standard as well as organic, will mean an extension to capacity in a year or so. Roland Allen sources his organic malts from North America, either from the US or Canada, but his hops are imported from England, Germany and New Zealand.

Organic Ale (4.8% ABV)

Ingredients: pale malt, caramalt and Munich malt. English Target, New Zealand Hallertauer and Pacific Gem, and German Spalter hops.
Tasting note: juicy malt and spicy, peppery hops dominate the aroma, with a firm-bodied malty palate balanced by tangy hops and tart citrus fruit in the mouth. The finish is long, with lush, creamy malt, bitter and spicy hops, and sharp fruit.
Availability: draught and bottled.

Organic Porter (6.5% ABV)

Ingredients: pale malt, caramalt, Munich malt and chocolate malt. English Target, New Zealand Hallertauer and Pacific Gem, and German Spalter hops.

Tasting note: black beer with hints of ruby, and a dense collar of barley-white foam. The aroma is enticing, with powerful wafts of chocolate, dark grain and spicy hops. Chewy malt, chocolate and hops dominate the palate, while the big finish is packed with luscious dark, creamy malt, chocolate, and dry, spicy and bitter hops.
Availability: draught and bottled.

India Pale Ale (7.1% ABV)
Ingredients: pale malt, caramalt and Munich malt. English Target, New Zealand Hallertauer and Pacific Gem, and German Spalter hops.
Tasting note: a vast aroma of ripe malt and peppery hops is followed by a palate dominated by bitter hops and citrus fruit, with good support from biscuity malt. The finish, long, lingering and complex, is dominated by a quinine-like hop bitterness with tangy malt; it finally becomes dry. At 7.1%, this beer is far closer to the style of the original IPAs brewed in Victorian England than is common in Britain today.
Availability: draught and bottled.

EEL RIVER

Eel River Brewing, 1777 Alamar Way, Fortuna, California 95540.
Tel 707 725 2739.
Email **eelbrew@northcoastweb.com** Website **www.climaxbeer.com**

Eel River is a brewpub run by Margaret and Ted Vivatson on the banks of the Eel River. The brewpub was built on the site of the historic Clay Brown Redwood Mill in Redwood Country in Northern California. The 30ft long bar was built from recovered Redwood and Douglas fir trees. Eel River's organic beer is made from imported malts, and hops from England and Yakima

Valley in Washington State: the American hops form part of the accepted five per cent of ingredients that do not have to be organic. The brewpub has an acclaimed restaurant and a shop.

Organic Amber Ale (4.75% ABV)

Ingredients: pale and darker imported malts. English and Yakima Valley hops (the English hops are not specified but are likely to be Target).

Tasting note: copper-coloured beer with a reddish tinge, and a tightly-beaded collar of foam. Rich aroma of juicy malt, spicy hops and citrus fruit (ripe blood oranges) and a hint of chocolate. Fruit and peppery hops dominate the palate, while the finish is sharp, tangy, with good hop bitterness and orange fruit. It finally becomes dry. Beautifully balanced, complex and refreshing. The beer is made in accordance with the California Organic Foods Act, 1990.

Availability: draught and bottled.

FISH BREWING

Fish Brewing Company, 515 Jefferson Street SE, Olympia, Washington 98501. Tel 360 943 6480.

Email **ch@fishbrewing.com/fishtail@olywa.net**

Website **www.fishbrewing.com**

Crayne Horton, founder of Fish Brewing, is a passionate man who champions the environment, using part of the proceeds from his brewery and adjacent brewpub to support environmental causes. He has helped, for example, to clean up of local water to aid the recovery of wild Pacific salmon. His labels and packaging state that his beers are brewed in the Republic of Cascadia: he and like-minded people in the Pacific North-west want to break away from the United States and form an independent republic that will also cover the neighbouring areas of Canada. Until that comes about, Crayne will concentrate on brewing organic beer and running the Cascadian Consulate and Cultural Center from the Fishbowl brewpub, where visitors can get their Cascadia Passport, which at the moment only allows them a tour of the brewery.

Amber Ale (4% ABV)

Ingredients: pale, crystal and Munich malts. New Zealand Hallertauer hops.

Tasting note: pale copper colour, with a pungent aroma of nutty malt, spicy hops and tart fruit. A big, full-bodied palate is dominated by tangy citrus fruit, juicy malt and peppery hops. The finish has creamy and nutty malt, balanced by bitter hops; it finally becomes dry.

Availability: draught and bottled.

River Run (4% ABV)

Ingredients: pale malt, rye malt, and torrefied rye. New Zealand Hallertauer hops.

Tasting note: pale bronze beer with a distinctive aroma of malted bread and lemon jelly. Chewy grain and spicy hops dominate the palate, while the lingering finish has a pronounced sherbet-lemon note, balanced by creamy malt. Torrefied rye, like any torrefied grain, is similar to popcorn and helps give a good head to beer. The beer is brewed in the spring in support of the fresh-water salmon the brewery is keen to help.

Availability: draught and bottled.

India Pale Ale (5.5% ABV)

Ingredients: pale, crystal and Munich malts. Centennial hops for aroma, New Zealand Pacific Gem for bitterness.

Tasting note: bronze-coloured beer with a superb tangerine and grapefruit aroma, more tart, tangy fruit and intensely bitter hops in the mouth, and a big finish dominated by citrus fruit, biscuity malt and quinine-like hop bitterness. A magnificent contribution to the revival of the true IPA style.

Availability: draft and bottled.

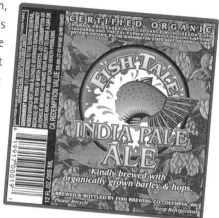

NB Fish Tale beers are certified by Oregon Tilth and the California Organic Foods Act. The Centennial hops in the IPA are not organic. Inspired by the success of Fish Brewing, there are plans to set up an organic brewers' guild in Oregon when other companies have acquired the necessary ingredients and certification.

LAKEFRONT

Lakefront Brewery Inc, 1872 North Commerce Street, Milwaukee, Wisconsin 53212. Tel 414 372 8800.

Email **info@lakefront-brewery.com** Website **www.lakefront-brewery.com**

Milwaukee is a famous brewing city with strong German roots. Schlitz, once the biggest brewery in the US, coined the marketing slogan "The Beer that Made Milwaukee Famous". Schlitz no longer exists, though its brands are produced by its once bitter rival, Stroh. The fall of Schlitz is an object lesson: in the 1970s, it attempted to undercut its rivals by cutting back on the barley and hop contents of its beer, saving 50 cents on each barrel brewed. In order to give the beer shelf-life and a foaming head, Schlitz added a stabiliser called Chillgarde. But Chillgarde reacted with another chemical in the beer called Kelcoloid (propylene glycol alginate), which encouraged flakes of protein to coagulate in the beer. When drinkers complained about being served "flaky beer", Schlitz removed the Kelcoloid. As a result, the beer went totally flat, without any foam. Sales nose-dived and Schlitz was taken over by Stroh.

Lakefront has attempted to turn the clock back to a time when Milwaukee had scores of craft breweries, before the rise of the national giants. The company was founded in 1987 by two brothers named Klisch, one of whom was a serving police detective. The brewery is in the downtown area of the city on the Milwaukee River. It's based in a former bakery and uses recycled brewing equipment. Three fermenting tanks are painted with the heads of Larry, Curly and Moe of The Three Stooges. The conventional beers include Pale Ale, German-style Dark and Pilsner, and such seasonal fruit beers as Pumpkin and Cherry.

In 2001, sales of Lakefront beers increased by 21 per cent to 4,437 barrels. As the Klisch brothers cheerfully admit, Anheuser-Busch, which produces 80 million barrels a year, spills more beer than they make.

Organic ESB (5.5% ABV)

Ingredients: pale, Munich and caramalt. German Perler hops.

Tasting note: copper-red beer with a rich malt, citrus fruit and spicy hop aroma. The full-bodied palate is dominated by orange and lemon citrus fruits, balanced by biscuity malt and tart hops. The big finish continues with biscuity malt, bitter hops and tangy fruit.

Availability: draught and bottled.

ESB or Extra Special Bitter is a popular beer style in the US, modelled on

Fuller's ESB in Britain. The Lakefront version has an identical ABV rating to Fuller's. The beer is certified by the Organic Crop Improvement Association.

WOLAVERS

Wolavers is based in Nevada City in Northern California, in the foothills of the Sierra Nevada mountains, and close to the Yuba River and Lake Tahoe. The company was founded in 1996 by Robert and Morgan Wolaver, passionate environmentalists, who market organic food and drink, and use part of the proceeds to support environmental causes. Posters and T-shirts they sell are made from recyclable materials, and they don't supply neon signs for their beers to bars.

Wolavers doesn't brew: the beers carrying their labels are available in 28 states of the union, making them comfortably the most widely available organic beers in the country. The beers are produced by three breweries: Goose Island in Chicago (www.gooseisland.com); Mendocino Brewing in Hopland, California (www.mendobrew.com); and Otter Creek Brewing in Vermont. As Wolavers (www.wolavers.com) referred enquiries to Otter Creek, the guide uses that company for details about the beers.

OTTER CREEK

Otter Creek Brewing, 793 Exchange Street, Middlebury,
Vermont 05753. Tel 800 473 0727.
Email **info@ottercreekbrewing.com**
Website **www.ottercreekbrewing.com**

Otter Creek was founded in 1991 by Lawrence Miller, a keen home-brewer who visited Europe to study classic beer styles and then established his own small commercial craft brewery in Middlebury in 1991. Success led him to move to a new site four years later. He has a 40-barrel brewhouse, and the quality of his beers are aided by the pure spring waters from the Vermont hills.

Wolavers Organic Brown Ale (5.7% ABV)

Ingredients: pale, Munich, caramalt, extra special roast, chocolate malt, and raw wheat. Hallertauer, Liberty and Tettnanger hops.

Tasting note: russet-coloured beer with a pronounced malt aroma balanced by tangy hops and dark fruit. The full-bodied palate has chewy, nutty malt with hints of chocolate and spicy hops. The finish is rich, creamy, fruity, with a good underpinning of spicy hops and tart fruit.

Availability: draught and bottled.

Wolavers Organic Pale Ale (5.8% ABV)

Ingredients: pale, Munich and caramalt. Cascade, Cluster and Hallertauer hops.

Tasting note: pale copper-coloured beer with a biscuity malt and citrus fruit aroma. Juicy malt and fruity hops dominate the palate and the long finish, which finally becomes dry.

Availability: draught and bottled.

Wolavers Organic India Pale Ale (6.6% ABV)

Ingredients: pale, Munich and caramalt. Crystal, Magnum and Hallertauer hops.

Tasting note: golden beer with a big, enticing aroma of rich juicy malt and citrus hop notes. The palate has biscuity malt, and lemon and grapefruit notes from the hops, while the long finish is superbly balanced between rich malt, bitter hops and citrus fruit.

Availability: draught and bottled.

Wolavers' beers carry organic certification from the states in which they are brewed.

NB American brewers are not required by law to state the strength of beer on labels or point of dispense. This is a hangover from the end of Prohibition, when the authorities decided consumers should not be told the strength of beer to stop them drinking the strongest liquors. Several craft brewers are now indicating strength but often use an American system called Alcohol by Weight, which can be confusing to drinkers in Europe. 2.5% weight equals 3% ABV, 3% weight equals 3.75% ABV, 3.9% weight equals 4.8% ABV, 4.8% weight equals 6% ABV. ABV is approximately 25% higher than Alcohol by Weight. The ABV ratings listed above are either declared by the brewers or have been divulged to this guide.

Chapter 8
Cider-making Methods

Most cider-makers use varieties of apples grown
specifically to be turned into alcohol. Outside the
West Country, some makers use culinary and dessert
apples, but most craft cider producers prefer the
hard, bitter, tannic and inedible cider varieties.

While there are "single varietal" ciders made from just one apple, most
ciders are made from a blend of apples to give the required balance of
flavours. Cider makers will choose from Bittersweets, which are low in acid
and high in tannin; Sharps, with a high acidity; Bittersharps, high in both
acids and tannins; and Sweets, which are low in acids and tannins. Culinary
or dessert apples on their own make a thin cider.

The fruit is harvested in September, and is then milled by a variety of
methods – usually by spiked rollers that crush the fruit into pulp. Next, the
juice has to be extracted in a cider press. As the pulp is difficult to handle,
it is laid on a cloth on the bed of the press and wrapped around and sealed.
Then layer after layer is built on top to a height of around four feet. This is
known as the "cheese". When the cheese is complete, a hydraulic jack
presses down on it and the juice runs out into collecting vessels.

The juice flows or is pumped into fermenting vessels. Some makers
prefer to allow the natural yeasts present in the juice to perform the
fermentation. Others, who want to produce brands with more consistent
flavours, kill the wild yeasts with sulphite and add a cultured wine yeast.

Fermentation lasts for several months. Left to its own devices, the yeast would turn all the sugars in the juice into alcohol, producing a bone-dry drink that many people would find unacceptable. A craft cider maker will stop fermentation when the desired balance of sweetness and dryness has been reached.

Cider usually undergoes two fermentations: the first one performed by yeast on the natural sugars in the juice, which takes place in the autumn; and the second in the spring during storage and maturation. This second fermentation is a malo-lactic one that converts malic acid into more gentle and acceptable lactic acid.

During this process, a substance called biacetyl is produced. This gives a buttery or butterscotch flavour to the aroma and flavour of the finished cider, and accounts for the "toffee apple" note found in some ciders in this guide. It is identical to the buttery note found in Chardonnay wine, and is not dissimilar to the diacetyl found in beer, especially lager, as a result of fermentation.

When fermentation is complete, the cider may be blended with older cider that has been stored for this purpose. This allows the maker to produce a finished product with the desired aroma and flavour.

Another substance present in apples is pectin, best-known as a setting agent in jam. Pectin is responsible for the haze in cider. At the end of fermentation and maturation, farm producers may simply sell cloudy cider at the farm gate. Many ciders are filtered to remove the haze. Cask-conditioned ciders, as with beer, are racked into casks and have some sugar added to encourage a further fermentation. A few bottled ciders are also packaged with live yeast, but most packaged ciders are filtered and artificially carbonated.

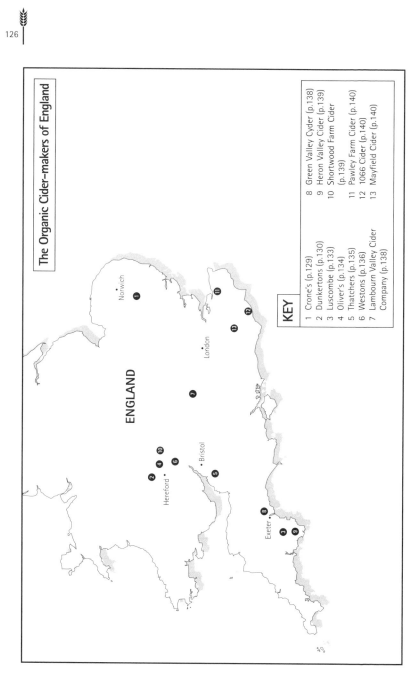

The Organic Cider-makers of England

ENGLAND

Norwich

London

Hereford

Bristol

Exeter

KEY

1 Crone's (p.129)
2 Dunkertons (p.130)
3 Luscombe (p.133)
4 Oliver's (p.134)
5 Thatchers (p.135)
6 Westons (p.136)
7 Lambourn Valley Cider Company (p.138)
8 Green Valley Cyder (p.138)
9 Heron Valley Cider (p.139)
10 Shortwood Farm Cider (p.139)
11 Pawley Farm Cider (p.140)
12 1066 Cider (p.140)
13 Mayfield Cider (p.140)

Chapter 9

Organic Ciders of England

Cider is one of the great historic alcoholic drinks of Britain. Climate changes confined cider-making to the West Country, the South-east and East Anglia, but at the dawn of history it was made throughout the British Isles.

It's thought that the Celts made a form of cider from crab apples, while the Romans in Britain regarded the apple and its fermented juice sufficiently seriously to create the Goddess Pomona to watch over them. The Romans developed sophisticated presses and mills to extract the juice from apples, techniques still in use today among some small traditional producers. While the Anglo-Saxons were important to the development of brewing in Britain, the ale-drinking Germanic tribes drove the Romano-Celts into the West Country, which explains – along with climate change – why cider-making today has its strongest roots in that part of England.

Cider-making and drinking flourished under Norman French rule, for Normandy was – and remains – a major cider-making region. For several centuries there was a considerable cross-Channel relationship between the cider-makers of England and France: such apple varieties as the Pippin were introduced to England from Normandy. Ironically, when England and France were perpetually at war in the 18th and 19th centuries, cider became a symbol of English patriotism. The aristocracy consumed it from fine cut-glass goblets, and toasted the downfall of the wine-drinking French.

The industrial revolution and the rise of a mass working class created a large commercial brewing industry to meet the needs of urban people engaged in heavy manual labour. Cider once again was confined to rural areas and became the drink of farmers and the labouring poor. Until the practice was outlawed, many farm workers had part of their wages paid in cider. Cider has maintained its popularity in the West Country and has enjoyed a national revival in recent years.

But as with beer, cider-making is now deeply divided between mass producers and smaller manufacturers. Many of the latter are based on farms, where cider-making is seen as part of the natural, seasonal nature of rural life. The small producers stand in stark contrast to such giants as Bulmer and Matthew Clark/Taunton Cider. Bulmer is the biggest cider-maker in the world. With Matthew Clark, it produces 90 per cent of all the cider made and sold in Britain. Both companies make small amounts of under-promoted traditional cider, but most of their production is geared to mass-market brands such as Strongbow, Dry Blackthorn and Woodpecker. Many of the national brands are made primarily with imported apple concentrate from as far away as Turkey, rather than English-grown cider apples. Such pale, carbonated drinks as Diamond White are aimed more at young lager drinkers than those that appreciate the true fermented juice of the apple. The smaller producers soldier on, supported by Camra, which features cider and perry at beer festivals, and publishes a regular Good Cider Guide.

Perry is made from pears. The best perry is the result of fermenting the juice of special varieties of the fruit that are so hard and full of tannin they cannot be used for any other purpose. True perry is not Babycham! The problem is that so many perry pear trees have been grubbed up in the West Country there is a serious shortage of fruit. It takes several years to grow new trees and for them to produce suitable fruit. Perry, the Champagne of the cider world, is in urgent need of consumer support.

As this guide was being finished, Bulmer announced it had withdrawn its organic cider. A drink marketed as "unpretentious", made from imported apple concentrate and put in a can failed to excite either drinkers or retailers. It proves just how badly a giant corporation can misread a specialist sector of the drinks market. To give Bulmer credit, it has worked with the Soil Association and Herefordshire farmers to convert 1,000 acres of traditional cider orchards to organic produce. These apples will be made available to other cider-makers, and Bulmer has not ruled out returning to organic production – hopefully in a bottle rather than a can, and using proper home-grown apples.

Craft cider-makers will produce dry, medium dry, medium sweet and sweet versions of their products by adjusting the blend of apples: some varieties have higher levels of natural sweetness than others, while others have more tannins. Big commercial cider-makers simply pour in sugar for sweetness. Under EU rules, small amounts of non-organic sugar, less than five per cent of total ingredients, can be used in ciders and perries labelled organic.

CRONE'S

Crone's Organic Cider, Fairview, Fersfield Road, Kenninghall, Norfolk NR16 2DP. Tel 01379 687687. Fax 01379 688232.
Email **info@crones.co.uk** Website **www.crones.co.uk**

Robert Crone was a cabinet-maker who started making cider as a hobby in 1984. It became a full-time business with his wife Jane. "From collecting wild scrumpy apples, we're now pressing 60-80 tonnes a year," Robert says. He produces around 5,000 gallons of organic cider a year. The Crones were joint winners of the 1998 National Cider Awards. They also have a sizeable business in apple juice and apple vinegar. Their organic apple juice has won an award in the Soil Association's annual food and drink competition every year since 1994. The ciders are fermented with natural yeasts on the skins of the fruit, and are cleared without the use of finings, making them suitable for vegans. A small amount of unrefined demerara sugar is added.

User Friendly (6.2% ABV)

Ingredients: Brown Snout, Dabinett, Kingston Black and Yarlington Mill.
Tasting note: rich, juicy apple aroma, with a bitter-sweet
palate and lingering finish that becomes dry.
Availability: draught and bottled.

Special Reserve (7.5% ABV)

Ingredients: Brown Snout, Dabinett, Kingston Black and Yarlington Mill.
Tasting note: sharp, tart aroma of bitter apples, a firm fruity palate of bitter-sweet fruit, and a long, dry finish with tart fruit and tannins.
Availability: draught and bottled.

DUNKERTONS

Dunkertons Cider Company, The Cider Mill and Cider House, Hays Head, Luntley, Pembridge, Leominster, Herefordshire HR6 9ED.
Tel 01544 388653.
Email **dunkertons@pembridge.Kc3.co.uk**
Website **www.dunkertons.co.uk**

Ivor and Susie Dunkerton are at the forefront of the cider revival in Britain (see Heroes of Organics). They founded their cidery in Herefordshire in 1981 and have planted new cider and pear trees. They started the trend to "single varietal cider" with Kingston Black, made from one apple variety, and in 1988 converted to organic production with the support of the Soil Association. Their apple varieties include Binet Rouge, Breakwells Seedling,

Brown Snout, Cider Ladies Finger, Tremletts Bitter, Roi de Pomme, and Yarlington Mill. They have planted orchards for such rare varieties as Bloody Turk, Kingston Black, and Sheeps Nose. In an attempt to save perry from extinction they have planted pear trees with such varieties as Barland, Blakeney Red, Butt, Moorcroft and Red Horse. Dunkertons produce 20,000 gallons of cider and perry a year. The cidery has been upgraded and modernised, and production is now in stainless-steel vats.

In 1994, the Dunkertons opened the Cider House, a restaurant and bar that offers their ciders, organic beer and wine, as well as good meals. As well as full meals lunchtime and evening, bar meals include Cider Maker's Delight with three British cheeses. Organic ingredients are used wherever possible. Draught and bottled ciders and perries are available from a shop on site, and the mill and orchards are open for visitors by arrangement. The Cider House is closed in January and February. For the rest of the year, opening hours are 10am to 5pm or dusk in winter, Monday to Saturday; dinner Thursday, Friday and Saturday from 7pm; Sunday lunch from 11.45am. Booking essential: 01544 388653.

Premium Organic Cider (6.8% ABV)

Ingredients: Brown Snout, Foxwhelp, Sheep's Nose and other organic apples.
Tasting note: Luscious fresh apple aroma with hints of toffee, sweet fruit in the mouth, and a finish that becomes dry but balanced by some residual sweetness.
Availability: bottled.

Traditional Dry (7% ABV)

Ingredients: Brown Snout, Foxwhelp and Sheep's Nose Herefordshire apples.
Tasting note: tart apple aroma, intensely dry fruit in the

mouth, with a tart, sour and quenching finish. Using different percentages of apples for sweetness and bitterness, this cider is also available in Medium, Medium Sweet and Sweet versions.

Availability: draught and bottled.

Black Fox (7% ABV)

Ingredients: Dabinett, Breakwells Seedling, Brown Thorn, Foxwhelp and Sheep's Nose Herefordshire apples.

Tasting note: sappy apple, leaf and stalk aroma, tart, refreshing fruit in the mouth, earthy, dry and bitter fruit finish. The cider is named after a mythical creature, a black fox, that has been seen for centuries on the England–Wales border but has always evaded capture.

Availability: bottled.

Organic Perry (7.5% ABV)

Ingredients: Merrylegs, Moorcroft, Painted Lady, Red Horse and Thorn perry pears.

Tasting note: pale gold, with a spritzy, minty, slightly herbal and gently fruity aroma, delicious bitter-sweet pears in the mouth, and a light but lingering finish with fruity, minty and slightly toasty notes, finally becoming dry. Superb.

Availability: bottled.

Improved Kingston Black (8% ABV)

Ingredients: Kingston Black Herefordshire apples: single varietal cider.

Tasting note: tart, dry fruit aroma, sour and vinous fruit in the mouth, with a long, dry, tart and bitter-fruit finish.

Availability: bottled.

Breakwells Seedling (8% ABV)

Ingredients: Breakwells Seedling Monmouthshire apples: single varietal cider.

Tasting note: Zesty fresh, earthy apple aroma, full-bodied fruit in the mouth, with a dry, juicy, rustic fruit finish. The apple variety was discovered in Monmouthshire more than a century ago and rescued for craft cider production.

Availability: bottled.

*Dunkertons, under European Union rules, may use small amounts of non-organic beet sugar, below 5% of the total agricultural content, in their ciders and perries.

LUSCOMBE

Luscombe Cider Ltd, Luscombe Farm, Colston Road, Buckfastleigh, Devon TQ11 0LP. Tel 01364 643036.
Email **luscombebeltd@freeserve.net** Website **www.luscombe.co.uk**

Luscombe means "Valley of the Swine" and happy pigs feature prominently on the cider maker's labels while one of the traditional cider apple varieties used is called Pig's Snout. Cider was added to the farm's activities more than 25 years ago. Local apples are crushed in a press on the farm, and then stored in oak vats before being bottled by hand. David Gabriel makes between 10,000 and 20,000 gallons a year. He uses natural yeasts for fermentation.

Organic Devon Cider (4.8% ABV)

Ingredients: Blend of Pig's Snout, Quench, Slack-ma-Girdle, Sops in Wine and Sugar Bush.

Tasting note: pale gold, with a tart fruit aroma, quenching fruit in the mouth, and a bitter-sweet finish.
Availability: bottled.

OLIVER'S

Oliver's Cider and Perry, Stanksbridge, Ocle Pychard, Herefordshire HR1 3RE. Tel 01432 820569.
Email **oliversciderandperry@theolivers.org.uk**
Website **www.theolivers.org.uk**

Tom Oliver is a relative newcome to cider-making. He started his company in 1998, produced 500 gallons a year but has increased production to around 1,500. He uses unsprayed fruit from Herefordshire orchards. It's good to see him making such an effort to help restore the image and knowledge of perry. As well as the regular products, Tom also produces single varietal perries, such as Blakeney Red, Long Red, Rabbit Foot, Toby Time, Coppy and Red Longdon when the fruit is available.

Medium Dry Cider (5.6% ABV)
Ingredients: Browns, Bulmers Northern, Dabinett and Tom Putt apples.
Tasting note: pale gold colour, with a bitter-sweet fruit aroma, tart and full-bodied fruit in the mouth, and a long tart fruit finish.
Availability: draught and bottle-fermented.

Medium Dry Perry (7.5% ABV)

Ingredients: blend of Balls Bittersweet, Blakeney Red, Collington, Foxwhelp, Hendre Huffcap, White Beech and Winnal's Longdon pears.

Tasting note: pale gold, gentle pear aroma, bitter-sweet fruit in the mouth, short but quenching finish.

Availability: draught and bottle-fermented.

NB The wholesaler for Oliver's ciders and perries is Richard Piggott, Winechooser, Brighton. Tel 01273 748672.

THATCHERS

Thatchers Cider Company Ltd, Myrtle Farm, Sandford, Winscombe, Somerset BS25 5RA. Tel 01934 822862. Fax 01934 822313.
Email **sales@thatcherscider.co.uk** Website **www.thatcherscider.co.uk**

William Thatcher started making cider on his farm in 1904 for his labourers. The business grew until cider-making overtook other aspects of farming, but the company is still run by the family, with chairman John Thatcher and managing director Martin Thatcher. (For those of a nervous disposition, the Somerset Thatchers are not related to You Know Who.) The company has invested £4 million in recent years on new production facilities, with state-of-the-art milling and pressing, plus a new warehouse and bottling hall. With five new Bucher Guyer presses, 15,000 tonnes of apples can be milled and pressed each season, enabling two million gallons of cider to be made each year. Thatchers is now one of the top five cider-makers in Britain, but it has avoided the tag of producing "industrial cider" and enjoys a good reputation among connoisseurs. Its products are widely available in pubs and supermarkets and it made a welcome entry into the organic sector in 2001. Visitors are welcome and cider can be bought from an on-site shop, open 8.30–6.00 Monday to Saturday, 10.00–1.00 Sunday.

Organic Cider (5% ABV)

Ingredients: Bramleys, Chisel Jersey, Dabinett, Kingston Black and Somerset Redstreak.

Tasting note: amber-gold colour, with a sharp fruit aroma with a hint of toffee (toffee apple?), with buttery fruit in the mouth, and a long dry finish with more hints of toffee.

Availability: bottled.

WESTONS

H Weston & Sons Ltd, The Bounds, Much Marcle, Ledbury, Herefordshire HR8 2NQ. Tel 01531 660233. Fax: 01531 660619
Email **tradition@westons-cider.co.uk**   Website **www.westons-cider.co.uk**

Henry Weston bought The Bounds farm in 1878 and two years later decided to make cider and perry for his family and his farm labourers. The red soil in the area is ideal for growing apple and pear trees. There was always a barrel of cider in the house for the family, while the labourers would bring wooden containers known as costrels to fill up from a hogshead in the cider house. A daily allowance of cider for years made up part of the workers' wages, until the practice was stopped by parliament. Henry Weston was encouraged to make cider and perry commercially by his neighbour, C W Radcliffe Cooke, the MP for Herefordshire. His enthusiasm for cider gave him the nickname in parliament of "the Member for Cider". Today Westons makes more than one million gallons of cider and perry a year, and is one of the country's top producers, but it has maintained traditional values alongside modern production methods. The products are matured in ancient wooden vats known as Pip, Squeak and Wilfred, bought early in the 20th century from a London porter brewery. Visitors are welcome and can tour the Cider Mill on Mondays, Wednesdays and Friday at 2.30pm. An on-site shop is open Monday to Friday 9.30–4.00, Saturday 10.00–1.00. Westons brands are on sale in most supermarkets and specialist shops such as Oddbins.

Waitrose Organic Cider (5.5% ABV)

Exclusive to the supermarket group.
Ingredients: Brown Snout and bitter-sweet varieties.
Tasting note: pale gold colour, light fruit aroma, bitter-sweet fruit in the mouth, tart and quenching fruit in the finish.
Availability: bottled.

Strong Organic Cider (6.5% ABV)

Ingredients: Brown Snout and bitter-sweet varieties.
Tasting note: autumn leaves colour, russet apple aroma with a hint of candy sugar, rich fruit in the mouth, and a bitter-sweet finish that becomes dry. The drink won the gold award for organic ciders in the International Cider and Beer Festival 2001, and Best Alcoholic Drink award in *You* Magazine/Soil Association Organic Food Awards 1998.
Availability: bottled.

Other Producers

The following cider-makers are small, often one-man operations. They say their products are made from unsprayed apples, but many of them do not have accreditation from the Soil Association or Organic Farmers & Growers as their volumes are too low and sales too restricted to warrant the expenditure.

BERKSHIRE

Lambourn Valley Cider Company

The Malt House, Great Shefford, Hungerford RG17 7ED.
Tel 01488 648441. Fax 08700 522514.
Email **lvc@westberks.demon.co.uk**
Website **www.westberks.demon.co.uk/lvcider**

Old Berkshire Perry (5.5% ABV)

Royal County Cider (6.5% ABV)

Kings Ransom Cider (6.6% ABV)

DEVON

Green Valley Cyder

Darts Farm, Clyst St George, Exeter EX3 0QH. Tel 01392 876658.

Traditional (7% ABV)

Standard Dry Cider (7% ABV)

Standard Medium Cider (7% ABV)

Standard Sweet Cider (7% ABV)

Rum Tiddly Tum (7-8% ABV)

Stillwood Vintage Dry (8.3% ABV)

Medium Sweet Table Cyder (8.3% ABV)

Heron Valley Cider Ltd
Crannacombe Farm, Hazelwood, Loddiswell, Kingsbridge TQ7 4DX.
Tel 01548 550256.
Soil Association accredited.

Ruddy Turnstone (6% ABV)

Heron Valley Farmhouse (6.2% ABV)

HEREFORDSHIRE

Shortwood Farm Cider
Shortwood Farm, Pencombe, Bromyard, Tel 01885 400205.

Bramley Cider

Organic Perry

KENT

Pawley Farm Cider
Pawley Farm, Painters Forstal, Faversham ME13 0EN.
Tel 01795 532043.

Dry Cider (8.4% ABV)

Medium Cider (8.4% ABV)

Sweet Cider (8.4% ABV)

SUSSEX

1066 Cider
3 Bedford Road, Hastings, E. Sussex TN35 5JS. Tel 01424 429588.

1066 Sweet Cider (5% ABV)

1066 Dry Cider (5% ABV)

Mayfield Cider
Pennybridge Farm, Mayfield, E. Sussex TN20 6QB. Tel 01435 873173.

Pennybridge Special

Donkey Kick

Chapter 10
Organic Ciders of France

Normandy is one of the great cider-making regions of the world. Unlike England, where most production is in the hands of two giant corporations, the French government encourages small producers by including cider in its AOC regulations for the production of wine and cheese.

AOC stands for Appellation d'Origine Contrôlée, a guarantee that a food or drink that carries the imprint comes from a designated region and reaches certain standards of production. Where cider is concerned, an AOC product must be made only from apple juice, with no added sugar or water, no apple concentrates can be used, and fermentation must be with natural yeasts (many English cider-makers kill natural yeasts and use wine or Champagne yeasts).

In the Pays d'Auge region of Normandy, where cider makers enjoy the protection of an AOC, even big cider producers, most of whose production goes to make Calvados, make some traditional ciders to the strictures of the government imprint.

In the 1960s, a group of local farmers in the Pays d'Auge, centred on the market town of Cambremer, formed the Cru de Cambremer to both promote and protect their tradition. They started to bottle-ferment their ciders, and this method has since become widespread.

Bottle-fermented ciders will improve and mature on their yeasts (*sur lie*), and will develop richer and more rounded flavours as a result. The region now has a Route de Cidre, with leaflets available from the tourist office in Cambremer, that directs visitors to all the cider farms. (Visitors should take with them the invaluable *Good Cider Guide* by David Matthews, Camra, £9.99.)

Production of cider is confined to so many small farms that sales are often restricted to local bars. Little is exported, and the quality is sufficiently high for many farmers to consider that organic production is unnecessary. But, with the French government encouraging people to consider the healthy aspects of eating and drinking, it is to be hoped that the makers of ciders of such stunning quality will consider it worth the effort to stop the use of chemical sprays on their trees and fruit.

CIDRE DE NORMANDIE

Domaine des Cinq Autels, 14190 Sierville-Bray.
Tel 0033 2231 781213.
Contact: Jean-Renée Pitrou.
The company is based about 15 miles south of Caen.

Domaine des Cinq Autels (5% ABV)
Ingredients: made only from organic French cider apples and certified by Agriculture Biologique.
Tasting note: pale gold, the cider comes in a 75cl bottle with a Champagne-style cork and cradle. It has a toasty aroma similar to Champagne, with tart, bitter-sweet fruit in the mouth, and a dry and toasty finish. It is beautifully balanced, quenching

and full tasting – a superb cider.
Availability: draught and bottled. Bottled version on sale in Britain via Unicorn Grocery.

CÔTEAUX NANTAIS FERME DES FRUITS

3 place Pierre Desfosse, Les Anjoncs, 44120 Vertou.
Tel 0033 2 440 755943. Contact Benoit Van Ossel.

This cider comes from southern Brittany and is a bi-products of an organic fruit farm. The cider comes in Brut (dry) and semi-sweet (demi-sec) form. As sugar cannot be used by law, French cider makers stop fermentation early to leave natural fruit sugars in the drink.

Brut (5% ABV)
Ingredients: organic French cider apples
Tasting note:g Golden colour with an aroma of tart and bitter fresh fruit, tangy fruit with a slight hint of toffee in the mouth, and a long tart finish.
Availability: draught bottled. Bottled versions available in Britain via Unicorn Grocery.

Demi-sec (5% ABV)
Ingredients: organic French cider apples
Tasting note: golden cider with an enticing and sappy fruit aroma, rich, slightly sweet fruit in the mouth, and a bitter-sweet, quenching finish.
Availability: draught bottled. Bottled versions available in Britain via Unicorn Grocery.

Chapter 11

The Heroes of Organics

The speed at which organic beer and cider are growing, especially in Britain, has brought many new producers on to the scene. They would not be making chemical-free drinks but for the pioneering work of a handful of iconoclasts in the late 1980s and early 1990s. We salute the heroes of organics, not only producers but also those who have fashioned bars and pubs where organic food and drink can be enjoyed by a growing number of discriminating consumers.

Singhboulton

Geetie Singh and Esther Boulton are passionate advocates of organic food and drink. Their first pub, the Duke of Cambridge in Islington, North London, is the world's first certificated organic pub. They have since opened a second in Victoria Park, Hackney, deep in the East End, and a third, the Pelican, in Ladbroke Grove, West London.

As they prepared to open the Pelican in 2001, Britain was mired in a farming crisis. The foot-and-mouth epidemic led to animal carcasses burning on funeral pyres from the West Country to the Scottish Borders. Coming in the wake of BSE, e-coli, and other disasters that resulted in part from factory farming and food processing, it was not difficult to grasp Esther's and Geetie's zeal for food and drink produced without agri-chemicals, and for a life-style based on renewable resources and localised production.

"The British are the biggest consumers of organic food in Europe," Esther points out, "but we are the lowest producers. In Austria and Sweden, ten per cent of food production is now organic, but in Britain we are importing so much and yet we have farming crises."

"Our policy is to buy British first, European second, and then go further afield," Geetie adds. "Isn't it absurd that we import lettuces from Zimbabwe when they're the simplest of all vegetables to grow?"

Esther and Geetie have been friends since childhood and have always worn their hearts on their sleeves. Both have been members of the Campaign for Nuclear Disarmament, and supporters of the Greenham Common protest against US air bases in Britain.

Geetie, from Worcester, trained for a year as an opera singer, dropped out, and has been working in the restaurant business ever since. "I just love everything about restaurants," she enthuses.

Esther is from Muswell Hill in North London, and had a peripatetic life in marketing, film, media and museum studies, but she also dipped in and out of the restaurant trade. Together they planned their first venture in 1997, at the Lansdowne pub in Primrose Hill, where they delighted in the good food and the informal atmosphere.

"We wrote a 60-page business plan, and looked for investment," Esther says. "We thought we'd raised the money to buy the Duke of Cambridge, but the bank pulled out and gave us less than three weeks to raise £100,000 from private sources." Investors included families and friends, and in 1998 the Duke, a failed, closed pub in an Islington back street, was theirs.

"People told us we were mad to choose Islington because of the intense competition in the area," Geetie says. "But there are actually very few small, independent restaurants, and the Duke is well away from the main eating places in Upper Street and Camden Passage. We have been busy since the day we opened."

The experience of buying and running their own business taught them a lot. As a result, they made fewer mistakes when they bought the Crown in Victoria Park. For example, they raised too much money for the Duke, and didn't make the same error twice.

The Crown, another formerly closed pub, seems at first sight an unlikely setting for an all-organic pub-restaurant. But this part of the East End is changing fast. It has access to the Docklands Light Railway and the Jubilee Line. Professional people are moving in, and property prices are shooting up. Opposite the main entrance to Victoria Park, a famous Cockney playground of grassland and lakes, the Crown has been busy and seems to have touched a chord in the area.

The Pelican is a street-corner pub in the cosmopolitan area of Ladbroke Grove, close to the famous Portobello Road street market. Dating from the 19th century, it has always been called the Pelican, a rare name for a pub.

The pubs are open-plan, with bare boards and scrubbed tables. The re-designs have involved the use of reclaimed building materials, and all the furniture is second-hand. Esther and Geetie describe the designs as "junkshop minimalist". All three places have a genuine pubby feel, with beer, wine and food chalked on blackboards. Both the Crown and the Pelican have upstairs rooms for more formal restaurant dining.

Caroline Hamlin, previously the chef at the Lansdowne, now cooks at the Crown, and has been the inspiration behind the menus at all three pubs.

The most notable aspect of the pubs is the enthusiasm and commitment of the staff. "We pay them well and give them good conditions," Geetie says. "We treat them ethically. We've never had to sack anyone."

"We don't need to," Esther adds. "If somebody is not up to scratch, it means they don't share our values. They leave if they don't fit in."

Geetie managed a health food shop for three years before starting the venture with Esther. "I had valuable contacts. If Caroline needs white organic flour, I know where to get it. When we started, there were a few organic wines, juices, cordials, Cognacs, bottled beer and draught Golden Promise. Then the Pitfield Brewery in Hoxton brewed a house beer for us called singhboulton, and followed that with Eco Warrior and a stout."

Now they sell organic gin and vodka, with wines from all over the world and four organic Champagnes. The beers include the Pitfield Portfolio, Freedom Organic Pilsener, and St Peter's Organic Bitter from Suffolk.

Geetie and Esther believe they face little direct competition, not because their food and drink is expensive – about ten per cent more than average pub fare – but because of the stringent demands made by the Soil Association, which regulates and certificates organic produce and outlets.

"If the government encouraged organic farming rather than agri-business, then prices of organic food and drink would come down," Esther says. "Localised farming would help cut out disease and the spread of disease," Geetie adds.

Consumers are responding to their vision, even if the government and the majority of farmers are not.

Duke of Cambridge, 30 St Peter's Street, London N1 8JT.
Tel 020 7359 3066.

The Crown, 233 Grove Road, London E3 5SN . Tel 020 8981 9998.

The Pelican, 45 All Saints Road, corner of Tavistock Road,
London W11 1HE. Tel 020 7792 3073.
Email **pubs@singhboulton.co.uk** Website **www.singhboulton.co.uk**

Caledonian Brewery

Edinburgh's Caledonian Brewery – known by the simple shorthand of "the Caley" – is the pace-setter for organic beer in Britain. Golden Promise was first brewed in the early 1990s, and was dismissed by a sceptical and conservative brewing industry as a nine-day wonder. But sales took off and the beer, draught and bottled, now enjoys substantial sales throughout the British Isles.

The brewery was founded in 1869 as Lorimer & Clark. It stands alongside the main railway line from Scotland to England, and it was bought in 1946 by the Vaux brewing group of Sunderland to supply a speciality known as Scotch to Vaux pubs in North-east England. Scotch is not whisky but a rich, creamy, malt-accented beer that was popular in particular with thirsty steelworkers and miners. Supplies of Scotch were taken by train from the Caledonian direct to Sunderland.

When heavy industry declined in North-east England, Vaux announced in 1987 that it would close the Edinburgh site. A buyout was organised by Russell Sharp, a former executive in the Chivas Regal whisky group, and Dan Kane, the Scottish organiser of the Campaign for Real Ale (Kane later died of cancer).

The newly independent Caledonian Brewery, with no pubs of its own to supply – it still has no tied houses – and a great deal of under-used capacity, struggled to find outlets in a country tightly controlled by Scottish & Newcastle, and the Bass subsidiary, Tennent Caledonian. The Caley achieved increased sales and production as a result of its devotion to good brewing practice, and restoring such revered Scottish styles as an 80/– Ale and the multi-award-winnning Deuchar's IPA [India Pale Ale].

The centrepiece of the brewery is formed by the burnished boiling coppers that are still heated by direct flame, once coal, now gas. According to Russell Sharp, direct flame ensures that the sugary malt extract and hops are "properly boiled and not stewed". Sharp's knowledge of malting from the whisky industry helped ensure that the finest grains were used in the beers. Caledonian now delivers beer to more than 500 pubs, while the success of Golden Promise has led to the company brewing other organic beers for supermarkets.

In 2001, after a long and exhausting period as managing director, Russell Sharp became president of the company, with his son, Dougal, in charge of brewing. The brewery has survived two major fires. On the second occasion, I was phoned by Scottish beer writer Allan McLean, who happened to be on a train leaving Edinburgh for the south, who yelled: "The Caley's on fire again!" Brewing continued among the smouldering ruins.

The company goes from success to success, with its own beer festivals, a memorable annual Burns Night supper, and invitations to visit the brewery and sup a few beers to players during Rugby Union internationals at Murrayfield: local wits claim that Caley invites the players from the opposing teams before matches and the Scottish players after them.

Caledonian Brewing Co Ltd, 42 Slateford Road, Edinburgh EH11 1PH. Tel: 0131 337 1286.
Email **info@caledonian-brewery.co.uk**
Website **www.caledonian-brewery.co.uk**

Martin Kemp

When Martin Kemp brewed a small batch of a beer called Eco Warrior in 1998, he had no idea that it would have a major impact on British brewing, and would turn his business upside-down. His Pitfield Brewery in Hoxton, North-East London, is tiny and can produce just a few barrels a week, but the success of Eco Warrior proved that small operations can have an influence that belies their size.

Martin has been involved in craft brewing since the early 1980s. In 1981, Brian and Elizabeth Brett set up a Lilliputian brewery in the basement of their off-licence, the Two Brewers, in Pitfield Street. The five-barrel equipment was installed by Martin, an engineer, and brewing was carried out by his old friend Rob Jones. A year later Martin and Rob bought the business from the Bretts and renamed the off-licence the Beer Shop.

In 1986 they moved the brewery to new premises, in old stables just round the corner in Hoxton Square. That year their beer Dark Star won the Best Small Brewery category at Camra's Great British Beer Festival and was runner-up in the Beer of the Year competition. One year later, Dark Star, from a brewery that cost £25,000 to set up and which produced just 25 barrels a week, won the overall title of Champion Beer of Britain in the Camra awards. At a time when a pop duo called the Beastie Boys were in the charts, Martin and Rob were dubbed the Yeastie Boys and revelled in their remarkable success.

But a couple of years later Martin and Rob decided to go their separate ways. Martin concentrated on retailing through the Beer Shop, while Rob brewed for a while in the Midlands before settling in Brighton and running a small brewery named, after his prize-winning ale, Dark Star.

In 1996 Martin moved the Beer Shop into bigger premises in Pitfield Street and had sufficient room to start brewing again. Space was cramped and he invited Rob Jones to build a similar plant to Rob's one in Brighton. It's based on the Russian doll system: the brewing vessels – mash tun, copper, and fermenter – are placed one inside the other, and are removed at successive stages of the brewing process. It's a brilliantly simple and effective method of making beer in a small space.

Martin brewed a Pitfield Bitter, now called Original, and gradually expanded his range. Then came Eco Warrior. It wasn't a truly organic beer at first, as Martin had difficulty sourcing his materials. But when a few newspaper articles (including one by the author in *The Guardian*) extolled its virtues, sales took off. Martin, in common with many other British brewers, found organic hops in New Zealand, while British maltsters started to meet the demand for organic grains.

The success of Eco Warrior prompted Martin to rethink his strategy. He realised that a tiny but influential section of drinkers wanted beers made without chemical fertilisers and sprays, and were prepared to pay the additional pennies to buy them. Today he has seven regular organic beers, he makes occasional beers for Halloween and Valentine's Day, and will brew special beers to order, as his plant can produce batches as small as 70 bottles. He makes a house beer, singhboulton, for the three London all-organic pubs runs by Geetie Singh and Esther Boulton.

Pitfield Brewery, the London Beer Company Ltd, 14 Pitfield Street, Hoxton, London, N1 6EY. Tel 020 7739 3701.
Website **www.pitfieldbeershop.co.uk**

Ivor and Susie Dunkerton

The Dunkertons are at the forefront of the organic cider and perry movement, passionate flag-bearers for food and drink made without harmful chemicals. Both of them gave up well-paid careers in London to settle in the West Country, and challenge the hegemony of near-neighbour Bulmers, the behemoth of the cider industry.

Ivor was a high-flying BBC television producer in the 1970s, working on such major programmes as *Panorama* and *Tonight*. Susie was working in theatre administration, and they had two young children to bring up.

"Working for the BBC kept me away from home a great deal of the time," Ivor says. "I was often in the United States and one day in New York I decided I was missing Susie so much that I was going to pack the job in.

"My colleagues couldn't believe I was turning my back on a career at the BBC, where promotion was a distinct possibility. Nick Ross, for one, told me I was mad."

But the Dunkertons sold their home in London and, with their two sons and Ivor's mother, then aged 90, they headed for Herefordshire. They settled in a 17th-century cottage near Pembridge, the area where they'd spent their honeymoon.

They extended the timber-framed building – "just to help them stay up!" says Ivor – and wondered what to do to earn a living on their surrounding 18 acres of farmland. They raised a few animals and thought of making goat's cheese, before Susie suggested producing cider. They had an immediate problem: the previous owners of their property had been teetotal and had grubbed up all the apple trees. But Ivor and Susie had a stroke of luck. Bulmers bought fewer cider apples that year – 1982 – and so the Dunkertons were able to buy apples at low prices from local farmers.

They realised there was no point in attempting to challenge Bulmers in the draught cider market. But neither did they want to emulate other small producers who concentrate on selling cider in takeaway containers at the farm gate. Ivor and Susie wanted to reach a wider audience. I first met them at an organic beer, wine and cider festival staged at Ryton Organic Gardens, near Coventry, where they became the centre of attention as a result of their passion for their products, helped by labels showing Adam and Eve as nature intended. Their cider and perry were sold in distinctive bottles, some with drawn corks. The message was clear: these ciders are as good as wine, and are made by craftsmen.

They make their cider and perry by pressing and fermenting the juice of separate varieties, storing them in cask, and then blending to produce different aromas and flavours. In recent years a new cidery has been built, with juice stored in stainless steel vats, but the aim is still the same.

"We're deep into flavour here," Ivor says. "Our ciders really taste of apples."

They decided to convert to organic production because they had seen at first hand – abroad as well as in Britain – the damage done to the enviroment by agro-chemicals.

"In the 20 years we've lived in Herefordshire, the wild life has been decimated," Ivor says. "Curlews and yellowhammers have disappeared completely, and I haven't seen a hare in years."

The Dunkertons buy apples and pears from local growers they have helped to convert to organic production. Ivor and Susie have developed their own orchards, stretching to 30 acres, with trees and fruit untouched by chemical sprays. Bird boxes nestle among the trees.

"Encouraging blue tits and other birds is vital as well as desirable," Ivor says. "They do as much to control insect pests as expensive sprays."

They have a Soil Association certificate and grow such apple varieties as Binet Rouge, Breakwells Seedling, Brown Snout, Cider Ladies Finger, Tremletts Bitter, Roi de Pomme, and Yarlington Mill. They have brought back such rare varieties as Bloody Turk, Kingston Black and Sheep's Nose.

Herefordshire was once so famous for its perry that the arms of the city of Hereford include pears. But the drink has gone into steep decline. Perry trees, difficult to grow and maintain, have been grubbed up by farmers looking for quicker profits, and the perry sector has been both dominated and distorted by Babycham.

On my first visit to the Dunkertons, they proudly showed me the pear tree saplings they were growing. Now they are bearing fruit, and such varieties as Barland, Blakeney Red, Butt, Moorcroft, and Red Horse have been restored. Dunkerton's Perry is sensational and it has won the accolade of Best Perry in Camra's National Cider and Perry Championships in 1998 and 2000. They have also picked up the Best Cider award in the 1999 Organic Food Awards, and Best Cider in the first Herefordshire Camra Cider Festival.

In the 1990s, Ivor and Susie opened the Cider House bar and restaurant in two 400-year-old cruck-framed barns, with flagstone floors and open log fires. Their ciders and perries – along with organic beer and wine – are on sale and are used in cooking. An organic herb and vegetable garden is being developed to supply the restaurant. The Cider House had to close in 2001 as a result of the foot-and-mouth crisis. It reopened at Easter 2002, a small but vibrant symbol of a different life-style that may yet save our wildlife and our environment.

Dunkertons Cider Company, The Cider Mill and Cider House, Hays Head, Luntley, Pembridge, Leominster, Herefordshire HR6 9ED. Tel 01544 388653.
Email **dunkertons@pembridge.Kc3.co.uk**
Website **www.Kc3.co.uk/business/dunker**

Robert and Morgan Wolaver

The Wolaver brothers come from farming stock, and they have returned to their roots to produce and sell food and drink free from harmful chemicals. They are now the biggest retailers of organic beer in the United States.

Robert Wolaver, the elder brother, moved to Hawaii in the 1990s to farm organically in an environment less damaged by intensive farming than mainland America. Morgan worked in the oil industry for several years, left that to join his mother in her real estate business, but quickly decided that kind of work didn't satisfy him.

"I wanted to get back to the grassroots of farming, the way my parents used to do," he says. "I joined Robert in Hawaii with the aim of setting up an organic food retailing company, but there were too many hurdles to go through.

"Then it dawned on us that there was no organic beer being brewed anywhere in the United States. We were inspired by Golden Promise from Britain, which was exported to the States."

Morgan and Robert explored the possibility of growing organic hops in Hawaii. The climate and the rainfall level were perfect, but the mountain slopes were too steep. Growing and picking hops would have been too labour-intensive to make economic sense.

So Morgan returned to the mainland, set up Wolaver's organic food and drink company in California, and looked around for brewers who could make organic beer. His pale, brown and India Pale ales are now made under licence by three breweries, but his main partner is Otter Creek in Vermont.

Morgan is determined to offer an alternative life-style in all areas of his retailing. He uses only recyclable materials, down to paper for wrapping, promotional posters, and coasters and drip-mats for his beer.

He plans to concentrate brewing at Otter Creek, which will merge with Wolaver's. Otter Creek brews conventional beers, but Morgan thinks founder Lawrence Miller will convert them all to organic materials. If the merger goes ahead, Wolaver's will close its California operation and move it to Vermont.

Wolaver's has bought an acre of land in the Yakima Valley in Washington State, the major hop-growing area in the US, and converted it to organic production. The land had to lie fallow for three years to get rid of fertilisers and pesticides. In 2001, Wolaver's contract brewers used half the crop, and Morgan expects to use the whole crop within a few years.

The success of the beers, on sale in 28 states, has prompted Robert to also quit Hawaii and help run the business. He and his wife tour the country in a mobile home-cum-office to sell Wolaver's beers.

Wolaver's, 409 Spring Street, Nevada City, California 95959.
Tel 001 530 478 0492.
Website **www.wolavers.com**

Otter Creek, 793 Exchange Street, Middlebury, Vermont 05735.
Tel 001 800 473 0727.

Pinkus Müller

When Johannes Müller and his wife Frederika Cramer opened their small brewery, bakery and chocolate shop in Münster in 1816, the ancient university city had 150 other beer-makers. Today Pinkus Müller is the city's only surviving brewery, and it remains small, producing a modest 10,000 litres a year. Yet it is famous throughout Germany and the rest of the world for the quality of its beers, and its dedication to organic production, using malts and hops free from chemical sprays.

The fifth and sixth generations of the family run the business. One daughter studied brewing at the brewing faculty at Weihenstephan University near Munich. The brewery has a tavern attached, where local cuisine is served with the beer. The tavern has four charming rooms, and the main dining area has a striking Westphalian oven in a tiled surround. Hams hang above a fireplace, and beams carry gilt-lettered mottoes about the pleasures of beer drinking.

The brewery was the first in Germany to convert to organic production. It buys Bioland-approved Gerstenbräu malt, and hops from the Hallertau region north of Munich. As a result of the brewery's pioneering work, increasing areas of the Hallertau are now set aside for organic production.

The most distinctive and curious beer brewed by the company is an Altbier: Alt, which means "old", is a speciality brewed in Düsseldorf, a warm-fermenting member of the ale family. The Pinkus version is a blend of malted barley and 40 per cent wheat, which is not true to the Düsseldorf style, but which is offered as an example of the "old" (pre-lagering) methods of Münster. This crisp and full-tasting beer is served in the tavern with a local syrup made from strawberries, peaches or oranges: the fruit cuts the acidity of the beer.

The brewery is best known abroad for its Spezial premium lager. It also produces a fruity wheat beer. It is a remarkable achievement for what is, in effect, a large brew-pub, to manage to make both cold and warm fermenting beers. But it is part of the family's dedication to quality, and to offering its interpretations of all Germany's traditional beer styles to an increasingly discriminating audience of drinkers.

Brauerei Pinkus Müller, 4–10 Kreuz-strasse, D-48143 Münster, Nordrhein-Westfalen. Tel 0049 251 45151, 0049 251 45152. Fax: 0049 251 57136

Email **info@pinkus-mueller.de**   Website **www.pinkus-mueller.de**

Chapter 12
Organic Pubs

The quality of food in British pubs has improved beyond all recognition in recent years as publicans have had to face the twin challenges of competition from fast-food restaurants and the demand from customers for more than just a quick pint and packet of crisps.

Many top chefs have left restaurants to accept the challenge of cooking quality dishes in pubs. Now a small but growing number of publicans have gone a step further and are offering organic ingredients in their dishes as well as organic beers, wines and spirits.

Duke of Cambridge

30 St Peter's Street, Islington, London N1 8JT. Tel 020 7359 3066.
Undergound: Angel

Website: **www.singhboulton.co.uk/duke.html**

The Duke is the first in the group of three pubs run by Geetie Singh and Esther Boulton that are totally dedicated to organic food and drink. The pub, built in 1851, has been carefully restored with wood floors, and some exposed beams and brickwork. The only noise in the pub is conversation, as there are neither music, nor TV, nor juke box, nor games machines.

There is a spacious bar at the front with smaller and more intimate areas at the back, reached by a corridor. As many as 40 small suppliers are used for ingredients, and this means the blackboard menu changes frequently, depending on what is available.

You may find pumpkin and sage soup; pork rillette, relish, pickles and toast; avocado, feta, tomato, chilli and mint salad; bruschetta with courgettes, tomato, feta cheese and olives; leek, ricotta and pine nut tart with mixed leaves and salsa verde; monkfish, mussels, clams, stewed with red pepper, potato, saffron, chilli and coriander; pan-fried sea trout, sauté potatoes, spinach, olives and lemon; roast chump of lamb with spinach, new potatoes and pickled red onion; grilled langoustines, fried potatoes, leaves and aioli; pumpkin, rosemary and parmesan risotto; Greek chocolate cake with crème fraîche; pear and date crumble with custard; watermelon sorbet with rum and lime.

The organic wine list is 40-strong, while the draught beers include Caledonian Golden Promise, Freedom Organic Lager, Eco Warrior and Shoreditch Stout from Pitfield Brewery in London – which also brews a house beer, singhboulton – and St Peter's Organic Ale from Suffolk. Even the cigarettes in the fag machine are organic, though I'm not sure this is a plus point. Food is served lunchtime and evening (not Monday lunchtime); menus change twice daily, and all dishes are available as children's portions.

Crown

233 Grove Road, London E3 5SN. Tel 020 8981 9998.
Underground: Bethnal Green.
Website: **www.singhboulton.co.uk/crown.html**

This spacious pub overlooks London's Victoria Park, a famous East End playground of lakes and rolling grass, a kind of Hyde Park for Cockneys. The downstairs bar is open-plan, but pillars act as dividers to create separate areas.

As well as scrubbed tables and chairs there are also comfortable Chesterfields. A long bar against the back wall helps create a genuine pubby atmosphere. There's also an upstairs dining room for more formal eating.

Menus lunchtime and evening may include red onion, puy lentil and thyme soup; home-cured bresaola, rocket and Parmesan; radicchio red wine risotto with Parmesan; smoked mackerel, horseradish, watercress and toast; slow-roast pork belly, new potatoes, fennel and prunes; boiled gammon with puy lentils, curly kale and parsley sauce; queen of puddings with cream; rhubarb fool with shortbread. Beers are the same as for the Duke of Cambridge.

Pelican

45 All Saints Road, corner of Tavistock Road, London W11 1HE.
Tel 020 7792 3073. Underground: Ladbroke Grove.
Website: **www.singhboulton.co.uk/pelican.html**

This is a compact street-corner pub with plain plate-glass windows giving good views both in and out – a sensitive touch, as many women find pubs with frosted windows and curtains intimidating. The downstairs L-shaped bar has plenty of comfortable tables and chairs while there's a small first-floor dining room.

The menu may include leek and parsnip soup; seared pigeon breast with roasted red onion, watercress and croutons; mushroom ragou with bubble and squeak; ham and parsley terrine with chutney, pickles and toast; roast tomato and peach salad with cumin, coriander and lemon; sea bass en papillotte with fennel and saffron potatoes; grilled swordfish with runner beans, roast tomatoes and chilli potatoes; venison and juniper stew with potato gnocchi; slow-roasted shoulder of lamb stuffed with anchovies, rosemary and garlic with oven-baked potatoes and herbs; braised artichokes with new potatoes, asparagus, broad beans and Gorgonzola; roasted apricots in dessert wine with marscapone; chocolate and cardomon cake with cream; spiced apple compôte with crème fraîche and shortbread; Plawhatch farm Cheddar, grapes and crackers. Beers are the same as for the Duke of Cambridge.

Castle

115 Battersea High Street, London SW11 3HS. Tel 020 7228 8181. Train: Clapham Junction.

This is a Young's pub with a real touch of chemical-free class – the organic meats include lamb raised on Prince Charles's Highgrove estate in Wiltshire. Landlady Gill Markwell doubles as chef, and her fast-changing menu may include parsnip soup; chicken breast wrapped in bacon and stuffed with Mozzarella, basil and roast peppers; herb pancakes stuffed with spinach, leeks and Stilton; warm goat's cheese salad with roast peppers; smoked chicken, crispy bacon and avocado salad; fresh salmon fillet on buttered leeks with Hollandaise; gammon in Madeira with parsnip mash; or spiced Moroccan lamb with apricots and cous-cous. Desserts may include chocolate pudding; spiced apple crumble or coconut ice-cream with cherry compôte.

Food is available lunchtime and evening (not Sunday evening). Mrs Markwell will cook vegan dishes to order where possible. The impeccable though not organic handpumped ales are Young's Bitter, Special and seasonal brews.

The spacious pub, with the air of a French farmhouse, and a garden for spring and summer drinking, stages live jazz on Wednesday nights.

Swan Inn

Craven Road, Lower Inkpen, Berkshire RG17. Tel 01488 668326.
Off A4, on Hungerford-Combe road.

The beers in the Swan are not organic but there is a strong emphasis on naturally produced food, as the owners, Mary and Bernard Harris, have their own organic farm that supplies the pub with beef and vegetables. The 16th-century inn has exposed beams, three open fires in winter and games room, and is close to Combe Gibbet.

As well as bar meals, there's an organic restaurant, while a galleried farm shop sells more than 150 items, including wines, ciders, fruit juices, eggs, cheese, cream, butter, chickens, lamb, and dried fruit, all from organic producers. Food in the pub is based around ten dishes a day, using organic meat, vegetables and fruit, and may include freshly-made sandwiches; soup; broccoli, mushroom and pasta bake; beef curry; home-made salmon, cod and smoked haddock fishcakes; steak in ale pie; ploughman's with organic cheese; beef in beer with Yorkshire pudding and fresh vegetables; leek and mushroom crumble; Boston bean bake with salad; bread-and-butter pudding; fresh fruit salad; and pear tart. There are cream teas in summer.

Draught beers include Butts Bitter and Blackguard from a small craft brewery in Hungerford, and Hook Norton Mild and Best, with guest beers and Lambourn Valley cider. Food is available lunchtime and evening. The Swan offers accommodation and is based in excellent walking country.

Blacksmith's Arms

Preston Le Skerne, Newton Aycliffe County Durham DL5 6JH.
Tel 01325 314873. 1 mile east of A167, on Aycliff-Great Stainton road.

Owner Pat Cook and her daughter are dedicated vegetarians and are keen to use as much organic produce as possible. As supplies are variable and sometimes unreliable, they have converted five acres of land next to the pub to grow their own vegetables, salad vegetables and fruit. They also buy vegetables from organic suppliers, and meat from a local butcher.

The duck, chicken, guinea fowl and peacock cheerfully roaming the pub grounds will definitely not appear on an eclectic menu that may include Caribbean scampi with coconut and fruit; beer rarebit; layered hot roast beef toasted sandwich with mushrooms, onion and fried egg; lamb braised in real ale with rosemary; Cajun spiced cod; lemon and coriander chicken; mushroom tart with potato scallops; steak and ale pie; curries; pasta dishes; and mixed plates for two including dimsum, Tex Mex and vegetarian. There's a thoughtful children's menu offering a dozen dishes with the likes of fishcakes, pizza, pasta in cheese sauce, and chicken dippers. Food is available lunchtime and evening (Sunday roast lunch; no food Sunday evening.)

Pat is also a passionate champion of small craft brewers in the North-east. The beers change every week, but you may find the likes of Hambleton Nightmare and White Boar, along with Black Sheep Bitter. Theakston Cool Cask is a regular.

Wenlock Edge Inn

Hill Top, Wenlock Edge, Shropshire TF13 6DJ. Tel 01746 785678.
On B4371, south-west of Much Wenlock.

The inn was fashioned from quarrymen's cottages at the turn of the 18th century. It has its own well, 190 feet deep, a wood-burning stove in an inglenook, and pews from a Methodist chapel in Liverpool.

Stephen and Di Waring offer a great welcome at this old inn, where they stage regular "tall stories" competitions. They use as much organic material as possible, with bread baked on the premises from organic flour, while both Double Gloucester and Shropshire Blue cheeses are organic, as are the sirloin steaks. Food in the bar and no-smoking dining room may include tomato and sweet red pepper soup; garlic mushrooms in sherry and creme fraîche; Loch Fyne hot smoked salmon; organic beef and mushroom pie; Shrewsbury lamb casseroled with vegetables, redcurrant jelly and Worcestershire sauce; cheese, leek and tomato flan; organic bean and vegetable bake; local leg of lamb with garlic and mint; Bakewell tart; apricot and almond sponge; and chocolate and orange mousse. There are splendid breakfasts for customers staying overnight.

Handpumped ales come from Hobsons, a small craft brewery in Cleobury Mortimer, which supplies Best Bitter, Town Crier and Old Henry. There are good wines by the glass and bottle, malt whiskies and proper ginger beer and lemonade. The inn has a herb garden and a wildlife pond, and is based in wonderful walking country.

Bottle Inn

Marshwood, Bridport, Dorset DT6 5QJ. Tel 01297 678254.
On B3165 between Crewkerne and Lyme Regis

Pub and village sit on the Devon/Dorset border. The inn is ancient, with the year 1585 cut above the door of the thatched exterior. Inside, there's an impressive inglenook with a cheering log fire in winter, a high-back settle, and other wooden furnishings. Landlords Sim Pym and Chloe Fox-Lambert specialise in organic and vegetarian food, along with organic beers, wines and ciders.

They will do their best to cater for people with special needs and food allergies. Dishes of the day (lunchtime and evening; closed Mondays November to Easter) are chalked on two boards, one for meat eaters, one for vegetarians and vegans. Dishes could include butterbean, garlic and parsley pâté; filled baguettes; ploughman's; pumpkin and coconut curry with rice, poppadom and chutney; homity pie; stuffed aubergines with spicy tomato coulis; Mata Paneer, an Indian dish made from tofu, peas, tomatoes and warm spices served with aloo sag and pilau rice; amd mushroom Stroganoff. Meat eaters can choose from leg of lamb stuffed with rosemary and garlic;

wild boar casserole; and chicken balti. Desserts include organic ice-creams, frozen organic yoghurts; and Dorset apple cake with Calvados.

The pub has two bars, with a family room and skittle alley, leading to a large garden overlooking Marshwood Vale. The inn hosts a nettle-eating competition in June – only organic nettles qualify. The beers usually include one from the Quay craft brewery in Weymouth, and Otter from Devon, along with the likes of Branscombe Vale, Fuller's London Pride and Wadworth 6X.

White Hart
Dartington Hall, Dartington Totnes, Devon TQ9 6EL.
Tel 01803 866051. Off A384, signposted Dartington

The White Hart is part of the Dartington Hall complex, where a bold experiment in switching to organic farming is under way: the complex includes three dairy farms and an organic market garden. The entire estate covers 1,000 acres, with 28 acres of landscaped gardens alongside the River Dart.

The inn, heralded by beer casks at the entrance, is part of the 14th-century courtyard of the hall that was built for John Holand, a half-brother of Richard II. Inside, there's an L-shaped room with a bar, log fires, stone floors and oak tables. Bar food is available at lunchtime and evening, and the menu is backed by a blackboard listing daily specials.

You may find filled baguettes; generous thick-cut sandwiches; gravadlax; pan-fried pigeon breasts with mustard dressing; red snapper in white wine sauce; organic Cornish lamb steak; or local game casserole. The desserts could include organic raspberries with cream. There are also local cheeses.

Beers come from the West Country and include Blackawton Bitter, Butcombe Bitter and Dartmoor IPA. The hall is based in splendid walking country, and there's a full programme of literary and artistic events. Children are welome in the restaurant and accommodation is available.

List of Stockists

Britain has a good range of stockists for organic beer and cider, ranging from national supermarket groups to small, specialist shops and mail order companies. Planet Organic in London is specially recommended for its wide range of organic drinks, as is the Pitfield Street Beer Shop. Vinceramos and Vintage Roots are long-standing suppliers of organic beer, cider and wine, while Unicorn is dedicated to organic food and drink. Among the nationals, Safeway has the best range of organic beer, while most nationals now have own-label organic brands. Selfridges, the leading London department store, has a good beer section. The specialist wine and beer group Oddbins carries a good range of beer.

SCOTLAND

Villeneuve Wines, 1 Venlaw Court, Peebles EH45 8AE.
Tel 01721 722500.
Email **wines@villeneuvewines.com**

Peckham & Rye, 155-159 Bruntsfield Place, Edinburgh EH10 3DG.
Tel 0131 229 7054.
Website **www.peckhams.com**

Peckham & Rye, 21 Clarence Drive, Glasgow G12 9QN.
Tel 0141 334 4312.
Website **www.peckhams.com**

Octopus at Fence Bay, Fence Foot Farm, Fairlie, Ayrshire KA29 0EG.
Tel 01475 568918.
Email **fencebay@aol.com**
Website **www.fencebay.co.uk**

NORTHERN ENGLAND

Barrels & Bottles (mail order), 3 Oak Street, Heeley Bridge, Sheffield
S8 9UB. Tel 0114 2556611.
Email **sales@barrelsandbottles.co.uk**
Website **www.barrelsandbottles.co.uk**

Beer Barons (mail order).
Email **mail@beerbarons.co.uk**
Website **www.beerbarons.co.uk**

Beers in Particular, 151 Highgate, Kendal, Cumbria LA9 4EN.
Tel 01539 735714.

Beer Ritz, 17 Market Place, Knaresborough North Yorkshire,
HG5 8AL. Tel 0142 386 2850.
Email **sales@beerritz.co.uk**   Website **www.beerritz.co.uk**

Beer Ritz, Arch Z, Granary Wharf, Canal Basin, Leeds LS1 4BR.

Dram Shop, 21 Commonside, Sheffield, S10 1GA. Tel 0114 268 3117

Flying Firkin, Hollins, Cowgill, Dent, Cumbria LA10 5TQ.
Tel 01282 865923.

Half Moon Wholefoods, 6 Half Moon Street, Huddersfield,
West Yorkshire HD1 2JJ. Tel 01484 456392.

Molly's Wholefood Store, 11 Front Street, Framwellgate Moor,
Durham DH1 5EJ. Tel 0191 386 2216.

Unicorn Grocery (mail order), 89 Albany Road, Chorlton, Manchester
M21 0BN. Tel 0161 861 0010.
Email **office@unicorn-grocery.co.uk**
Website **www.unicorn-grocery.co.uk**

Vinceramos (mail order), 261 Upper Town Street, Leeds LS13 3JT.
Tel 0113 257 7545.
Email **info@vinceramos.com**
Website **www.vinceramos.com**

York Beer Shop. 28 Sandringham Street, Fishergate, York YO1 4BA.
Tel 01904 647136.

CENTRAL ENGLAND

Bottle Store, 77 Queens Road, Leicester LE2 1TT. Tel 0116 270 7744.

Growing Concern, Home Farm, Woodhouse Lane, Nanpantan, Loughborough, Leictershire LE11 3YG. Tel 01509 239228.

Henry Doubleday Research Association, Ryton Organic Gardens, Ryton-on-Dunsmore, Coventry, CV8 3LG. Tel 01203 303517. Shop and restaurant.

Louth Wholefood Co-Op, 7-9 Eastgate, Louth, Lincolnshire LN11 9NB. Tel 01507 602411.

Small Beer, 199 Grimsby Road, Grimsby, Lincolnshire DN35 7HB. Tel 01472 699234. Email **dave@sbclle.freeserve.co.uk**

Small Beer, 91 Newland Street West, Lincoln LM1 1QF. Tel 01522 528628.

Wholefood Co-Op, 27 Osborne Street, Grimsby, Lincolnshire DN31 1EY. Tel 01507 251112.

EASTERN ENGLAND

Wisbech Wholefoods, 8 North Street, Old Market, Wisbech, Cambridgeshire PE13 1NP. Tel 01945 464468

HOME COUNTIES

Cook's Delight, 360/364 High Street, Berkhamsted, Hertfordshire HP4 1HU. Tel 01442 863584.

Swan Inn & Organic Beef Company, Craven Road, Inkpen, Hungerford, Berkshire, RG17 9DX. Tel 01488 668326

Vintage Roots, Farley Farms, Bridge Farm, Reading Road, Arborfield, Berkshire RG2 9HT. Tel 0118 976 1999.

LONDON

Beer Shop and Pitfield Brewery, 14 Pitfield Street, London N1 6EY. Tel 020 7739 3701.
Wesbite **pitfieldbeershop.co.uk**

Food Brands Group, 9-10 Calico House, Plantation Wharf, Battersea, London SW11 3TN. Tel 020 7978 5300.

Planet Organic, 42 Westbourne Grove, London W2 5SH. Tel 020 7221 7171 or 020 7727 2227. Deliveries/mail order tel 020 7221 1345.
Email **deliveries@planetorganic.com**

Planet Organic, 22 Torrington Place London WC1 7JE. Tel 020 7436 1929. Deliveries/mail order tel 020 7221 1345.
Email **deliveries@planetorganic.com**

Premier Beer Imports, 204 London Road, Hackbridge, Surrey
SM6 7EA. Tel: 020 8669 7051.
Importers of beers, including Irish brewer Celtic Brew.

Ravensbourne Wine, Unit 6.0.2 Bell House, 49 Greenwich High Road,
London SE10 8JL. Tel 020 8692 9655.

SOUTH-EAST ENGLAND

Finbarr's Wholefoods, 57 George Street, Hastings, East Sussex
TN34 3EE. Tel 01424 443025.

Organic Health (Perry Court), The Well House, Perry Court Farm,
Garlinge Green, Canterbury, Kent CT4 5RU. Tel 01227 732563.

Sedlescombe Vineyard, Cripp's Corner, Sedlescombe,
Nr Robertsbridge, East Sussex TN32 5SA. Tel 01580 830715.
Website **www.tor.co.uk/sedlescombe**

WALES

Irma Fingal-Rock, 64 Monnow Street, Monmouth NP5 3EN.
Tel 01600 712372.

Maethy Meysydd, 11 Princes Street, Aberystwyth, Ceredigion
SY23 1DX. Tel 01970 612946.

Old Butcher's Shop, Broad Street, Montgomery, Powys SY15 6NP.
Tel 01686 668229.
Email **onlyorg@montgom.demon.co.uk**

Quarry Shop, 21 Maengwyn Street, Machynlleth, Powys SY20 8EB.
Tel 01654 702624.

WEST COUNTRY

Natural Collection, 19A Monmouth Place, Bath, Somerset BA3 6LP.
Tel 01225 442286.

USA

Seven Bridges Cooperative, 419 May Avenue, Santa Cruz, CA 95060.
Tel 001 800 768 4409 / 001 831 454 9665. Fax 001 831 466 9844.
Email **7bridges@breworganic.com**

See the annual *Organic Directory*, c/o Green Books Ltd, FREEPOST
(EX2335), Devon, TQ9 6BR.
Website **www.mamba.demon.co.uk/organics**

Select Bibliography

Recommended further reading:
Organic: A New Way of Eating by Sophie Grigson and William Black, Headline, £25.
Fast Food Nation by Eric Schlosser, Penguin Books, £6.99.
Silent Spring, Rachel Carson, Penguin Books, £7.99.
The Sea Around Us, Rachel Carson, Oxford University Press, £7.99.
Rachel Carson: Caring for the Earth, Elizabeth Ring, Gateway, £6.83.
Small is Beautiful, E F Schumacher, Vintage, £7.99.
Good Cider Guide, David Matthews, Camra, £9.99.
Good Beer Guide, Roger Protz, Camra, £12.99 (updates the British brewing industry annually)

Useful contacts

The Soil Association website: **www.soilassocation.org**
Membership of the association is open to individuals, not just farmers or companies.

Campaign for Real Ale (Camra). Website: www.camra.org.uk.
Up-to-date information on the British brewing industry. Membership includes a monthly newspaper, *What's Brewing*. Tel 01727 867201.

www.realbeer.com International beer site, including
www.protzonbeer.com

Index

Beers featured in this book appear in **bold** type